"LOVE, LOVE, LOVE this book. This is my new manual on how to live my life. It makes complete sense. Thank you!!"

Sue Edwards, Nambour, AUSTRALIA

"Brilliant! HOW LIFE WORKS exceeded my expectations... and then some! I can open to any page and discover new ways to make my life better."

Bill Swan, Victoria, CANADA

"HOW LIFE WORKS is your best book yet! For me it is the missing link. I haven't felt this good in years."

Michael Higgins, Brisbane, AUSTRALIA

"Andrew Matthews' best book yet. Five Stars!"

Gary Moon, Washington, USA

"Great tips for simple steps, simple changes. Awesome advice, that sets a great path forward. This rocks. So will you. It's all here. Love it. :)"

Karen Jane Nuttall Pike, Auckland, NEW ZEALAND

"Incredible book. HOW LIFE WORKS is the instruction manual for life that we should be given at birth."

Dr Wendy Shauer. Washington, USA

READERS' COMMENTS

"I never thought self-help books were for me but, whoa, how wrong I was! Your books are easy, fun, enjoyable. I can apply these things EVERY DAY.

I can't believe how my life has changed in all areas. I even landed my dream job with a major airline at 44! Thank you, thank you! You rock!"

Andy Jackson, Auckland, NEW ZEALAND

"Your books changed my life when I was 16 years old and going through depression. Now, I'll always be okay! Thanks so much!"

Linda Lu, Valparaiso, CHILE

"Before I was introduced to your books I relied on other people and other things to make me happy. I went through bouts of alcohol and drug abuse, went to therapy and had to take anti-depressants."

"Now having read your books three years ago I have realised I do deserve happiness and success and I am experiencing it for the first time."

Nancy Hayes, Alaska, USA

"Your books are helping me as a kind of miracle in all of my hard times. They have changed my life – and they have changed my friends' lives. I really love them!"

Omid Mortazavi, IRAN

"I've read hundreds of personal development books. All of them combined don't give me the inspiration, insight and peace of mind of Andrew Matthews' books. They saved my life. I have achieved more in 1 month than in 40 years!"

Peter Thompson, U. K.

HOW
LIFE
WORKS

written and illustrated by
Andrew Matthews

WATKINS
Sharing Wisdom Since 1893

First published 2014 by Seashell Publishers
This edition first published in the USA 2018 by
Watkins, an imprint of Watkins Media Limited
19 Cecil Court
London WC2N 4EZ

enquiries@watkinspublishing.com

1 3 5 7 9 10 8 6 4 2

Printed and bound in the United Kingdom

A CIP record for this book is available from the British Library

ISBN: 978-1-78678-172-7

www.watkinspublishing.com

Also by the same author:
Being Happy!   **Happiness Now**
Making Friends   **Happiness in Hard Times**
Follow Your Heart   **Stop the Bullying!**
Happiness in a Nutshell   **Being a Happy Teen**

THANK YOU
To Julie, my wife

You are amazing.

Thank you for your love and guidance.

Thank you for all you have done over twenty years to take our books to the world. Nobody knows how hard you have worked or the sacrifices you have made.

I am in awe of your vision, your courage, your persistence and your generosity. I am blessed daily by your beautiful spirit.
I love you.

To Ian Ward

Thank you for publishing my first book, *Being Happy!*
When no other publisher wanted my raw manuscript, you and Norma gave me the chance of a lifetime. I am so grateful to you for your foresight, your generosity and your relentless commitment. You changed my life.

To Caroline Dey

Thank you for your interest in this book from the beginning – and for your many helpful suggestions. Thank you for being my friend for thirty years and for always making me laugh.

To Dr George Blair-West

For your friendship, for our countless sessions on Skype and your good advice – thank you buddy!

To Juergen Schmidt

Thank you for sharing your wisdom –
and thank you for your encouragement.

Contents

When Bad Things Happen

1

Late one night Trent was cruising down the highway when a stray cow decided to cross the road. Trent swerved but hit the cow head-on. His car rolled. The cow died.

Trent survived. Trent fixed his car. But his troubles weren't over …

Trent needed to relax. He went fishing and cut his foot on a rock. It was a small cut but it wouldn't heal. To be safe, Trent saw a doctor. The doc said, "Forget it! It is only an inflamed tendon." But when his right foot became the size of a watermelon, Trent sought a second opinion. The surgeon told him, "You have a massive infection. You might lose your leg."

Trent spent the next ten days in hospital. They saved his leg.

Back at work, Trent was driving down a country road and rounded a corner to discover an out-of-control Toyota Corolla on the wrong side of the road coming straight at him. Trent hit the brakes – and the Corolla.

Trent survived, but his troubles weren't over …

Trent had gotten some financial advice. He invested all his money with a company called Storm Financial. Everything was perfect – until the Global Financial Crisis, when Storm Financial hit the perfect storm. Trent survived, but Storm Financial didn't.

Trent lost his life savings.

Trent's story is your story and my story. Why do bills and bad drivers come in bunches?

Do we have control over seemingly random events, or is life a lottery of stray cows and rampant bacteria? We'll get to this shortly …

When Good Things Happen

Jane is thirtyish and single. All her girlfriends have boyfriends or husbands. Jane wanted one, too. She wondered, "What is wrong with me?"

Finding a man became her obsession. Whenever she walked into a supermarket or an elevator or onto a plane, she would ask herself, "Will he be here?"

He never was.

Whenever she did have a date, it evaporated. The guy got pneumonia and cancelled. The guy's Italian grandmother had a heart attack and he left the country. Jane tried internet dating and hated it. Finally, she had had enough. She told herself, "I don't need a man. I'll do some study. I'll get a dog!"

She joined an online Chinese language class. She reconnected with old girlfriends. She went to the theatre. She started enjoying life. She bought a puppy.

And you can guess the rest. The day she ditched the idea of a boyfriend, men began showing up by the truckload.

- A handsome neighbour rescued her puppy from the stairwell and took her out for coffee
- A friend from high school – complete with the *"I'm just divorced and you are the only girl I ever loved"* routine – tracked her down on Facebook
- Her landlord's brother came to change a light bulb and stayed for breakfast.

She wasn't looking; she wasn't even trying. She never spent one minute in a seedy bar. It just happened.

Why is it that when good things happen, more good things happen?

Is It a Coincidence?

Does this ever happen to you?

- You are about to phone someone you haven't called in a month when suddenly she calls you
- You hear about an interesting book and decide you want to read it. Next day you walk into a friend's house, or a junk shop, or you step onto a train, and there it is
- You start humming an old song – and then turn on the radio, and it's playing.

Or this?

- You are out on a date, and you have the thought, "I would really hate to meet my ex-husband!" You walk into the restaurant, and there he is with his new fiancée
- You buy a new car and tell yourself, "I hope I don't scratch it." Within twenty-four hours some kid demolishes your tail light with a runaway shopping cart
- You spend a year planning a skiing vacation. You tell yourself, "I hope I don't get sick!" You catch the 'flu on the flight out and spend the week in your hotel room.

We may explain these things away as coincidence. It's more than that.

Quantum physics has now proven what spiritual masters have taught for three thousand years: thought affects matter, and everybody and everything is connected.

Thoughts are real things. Your thoughts create your circumstances. But that is only half the story. What matters most is how you FEEL.

This book is about why GOOD THINGS HAPPEN WHEN WE ARE FEELING GOOD, why BAD THINGS HAPPEN WHEN WE ARE FEELING BAD – and how to feel better so that more good things happen.

In the process you may get some insight into:

- why bad things sometimes happen to good people
- why placebos work and diets don't
- why rich people make money – even by accident
- why Jane now has boyfriends coming out her ears.

Whether you get the job of your dreams, whether you stay healthy, or whether you find your perfect life partner depends on how you FEEL.

How Life Works may confirm what logic told you is impossible, but a part of you always knew.

Your life is not a lottery. It never has been.

The Red BMW

When I was twenty-six, I drove an old Datsun 180B. I wanted a nice car and I had a budget of $10,000.

I had friends who stuck photographs of their goals on their refrigerators. They told me, "What you plant in your subconscious mind you attract." So I cut out a colour picture of a bright red 320i BMW from a magazine and stuck it on the wall above my desk at home. Nobody saw it. I told no-one about the car I wanted. From time to time I imagined how it would feel to drive a 320i, but I did nothing about it.

A few weeks later I was in a coffee bar chatting with my buddy, Steven. He loved cars. He asked me, "Why don't you get yourself a decent set of wheels?"

I said, "I'm planning to."

But I never told him what car I wanted or what my budget was.

A month went by, and I bumped into Steven. He said, "There's a great little car for sale in a yard in Franklin St."

I said, "What is it?"

He said, "A BMW."

Now he had my interest. "What model?"

"320i."

"What colour?"

"Bright red."

"How much?"

He said, "It's $11,500 but you could offer $10,000."

My eyes almost popped out of my head. I thought, "This is weird!"

I bought the car for $10,000 – and figured the whole thing was a coincidence. After thirty years of watching these things happen – and studying people who make things happen – I know it wasn't.

Hundreds of books have been written about the power of the subconscious mind, including *Think and Grow Rich*,[1] *Psycho Cybernetics*,[2] *The Magic of Believing*[3] and *The Power of Positive Thinking*.[4]

The message in all these books is that thought is creative, and the more you think about something – whether you want it or whether you don't – the more likely it is to happen.

So how does the subconscious work? And how important is belief?

Let's take a look …

What Controls Your Life

2

Is this typical?

- Mary goes on the latest Hollywood diet
- Mary loses ten kilograms in ten weeks and looks sensational
- Mary piles on ten kilograms in the next six weeks
  and looks like the usual Mary.

Why is that? Because her subconscious mind is in control. And so is yours.

You can starve yourself with willpower. You can eat grapefruit or even grass. You can lose 50 kilograms. But until your subconscious accepts *"I am slim"*, all weight loss is temporary.

In a battle between willpower and your subconscious mind, your subconscious will always win.

So How Powerful Is the Subconscious?

Every night when you go to sleep, you continue breathing, your heart keeps pumping and you continue digesting dinner. So what is controlling all that? And what stops you from wetting the bed? It's your subconscious mind.

Ninety-nine percent of your brain power is in that part of your mind of which you are not aware.

Amazing, isn't it? You can drive a car while munching peanuts, singing to the radio and planning dinner. Every few seconds you steer, brake or accelerate while giving no thought to controlling the car. So who is doing the driving?

It's your subconscious.

One Big Recorder

If you ask a touch typist, "Where are all the letters on your keyboard?" she'll probably have no idea! She can punch out 80 words per minute blindfolded, but she can't TELL you where the keys are – until she starts typing.

Why? The keyboard is in her subconscious.

Your subconscious mind is one giant recorder. It has programs you were born with – that regulate your breathing, your heartbeat and a thousand other bodily functions – and it has programs you created – like how to walk, talk, type, dance, drive and whistle.

It is easiest to create *new programs* before you are six years old.

Why Children Learn So Fast

Children's brain waves are different; they are slower, and that is why children live in the present moment. Until you are about six, you are an open book, effortlessly downloading information.

Children have no adult conscious mind saying, *"This is too hard."* That's why three-year-olds pick up Russian or Chinese without effort; it's why four-year-olds learn to snow ski in three hours.

Children have no filters, no barriers. This explains why you can retard a little child for life by telling him he is stupid. Whatever you tell a four-year-old – "You are beautiful", "You are special", "You are a loser", "You make Mummy unhappy" – becomes law for him.

The subconscious explains a lot of bad behaviour. You let a four-year-old play endless computer games with kicking, punching and swearing – and watch movies with kicking, punching and swearing – and you create a brat. There is no adult conscious mind to filter what is *okay for a movie* and what is *not okay for real life*. The behaviour is simply downloaded. Then we blame the kids.

THE SUBCONSCIOUS MIND DOESN'T ARGUE. IT JUST ACCEPTS INFORMATION AS FACT.

"I Just Want to Do Nothing"

Your subconscious mind takes instructions very literally.

Nicole planned a vacation in Bali. She told me, "In the months before my Bali trip, I kept telling myself, 'All I want to do is lie down and do nothing'."

I asked her, "How was Bali?"

She said, "I got a five-day migraine that transformed into the 'flu. I spent the whole week in my hotel room doing nothing."

Two years later Nicole returned to Bali. She explained, "I still didn't understand that I had helped to create my illness. So before the second visit I kept telling myself, 'When I get to Bali, I want to lie down and do nothing'." So how was Bali?

She told me, "I caught a parasite on day one; I couldn't eat, couldn't drink, couldn't read, couldn't even sit up. I spent five days in hospital on a drip doing absolutely nothing."

When you plant a thought, your subconscious delivers.

Nicole wasn't finished with Bali. She says, "For my third vacation I had a new strategy. I visualised my perfect holiday ahead of time. I saw myself healthy and my children healthy. I imagined us happily plunging down waterslides, relaxing by the pool, enjoying great shopping and wonderful food.

"Finally, we had the perfect vacation."

ANDREW MATTHEWS

Your Subconscious and Money

William "Bud" Post won 16 million dollars in the Pennsylvania State Lottery. Bud's brother hired a hit man to kill Bud so he could inherit it (Bud survived), his ex-girlfriend sued him for a chunk of it, and his family hounded him for the rest of it.

Within a year Bud was a million dollars in debt. Bud might argue, "My problem is my relatives!"

But seven out of ten lottery winners lose the lot.

> If you win ten million dollars you are just a temporary millionaire.

If you win ten million dollars you are just a *temporary* millionaire. Whether you stay rich has little to do with clawing relatives or global financial crises. It has everything to do with your subconscious.

In a Nutshell

Your beliefs will eventually triumph over willpower.

Why Do the Same Things Keep Happening to Me?

3

Patterns

Have you noticed that some people are always broke? You can hand them $10,000 cash, and before you know it they need a bank loan to buy a pizza.

Some people are always late! They can get up at 6 am to be at work by nine and at ten fifteen they are still combing the house for car keys and hunting for their wallet!

Some people are always busy.

Some people are forever getting ripped off – by salesmen, phone companies, old girlfriends and long-lost relatives.

Did you ever meet a lady who said, "I always end up dating jerks."? She has a radar for finding rude, selfish, lazy people – and then she marries them.

Some people start a new relationship every six weeks.

ANDREW MATTHEWS

"I need space."

ANDREW MATTHEWS

To get it, you have to feel it.

Some people make friends wherever they go. Some people make money wherever they go.

Some people have fun wherever they go. Some footballers are always where the ball is.

Some people always land on their feet. Their pattern says, *"Things always work out."* Ted's car breaks down in the middle of nowhere, and a stranger picks him up, drives him home and then offers him a job!

Subconscious patterns are why history repeats itself. So, for example, Mary always finds wonderful jobs but never finds faithful boyfriends. Bill never gets sick but keeps getting the sack!

None of this is coincidence. We each attract – and create – our life experiences through our subconscious programs.

You say, "If your subconscious patterns create your life, there would be happy people who sail from one adventure to another and miserable people who stagger from one disaster to another.

"And some people would keep getting richer, and some people would keep getting poorer!"

That is how it is. That is how it has always been.

In a Nutshell
Life unfolds from the inside out.

The Good News
Here's the good news: you are not your patterns and YOU CAN CHANGE YOUR PATTERNS.

For life to get better, you don't need to dwell on how you created your past. You don't need to worry about what you did "wrong".

You just need to understand that you helped create it and begin to think and feel differently.

"I've got a headache."

How We See Ourselves

4

If you survey people in a shopping mall and ask them, "Are you generous?", even people who never ever gave a cent to a charity or a panda will tell you, "Sure I'm generous." Nobody thinks they are mean!

Ask anyone, "Have you got a sense of humour?" Everybody has! When did you ever meet someone who said, "I don't know what's funny."?

And every guy thinks he is a great driver!

We see ourselves as we want to see ourselves.

So if you ask people, "Are you positive?", most people think they are positive. They say things like, "I'm positive. It's my stupid husband that's the problem!"

> *"I'm positive. It's my stupid husband that's the problem!"*

Negative people don't think they're negative. They think they are *realistic*.

Most of us grew up with worried parents who taught us to worry. They told us what we couldn't have, what we couldn't do and what we would never be. The nightly news confirmed that the world is a dangerous place.

How on earth could we become fearless, free spirits?

In a Nutshell
For most of us, negative became normal.

Negative Rats
Many people seem happy and positive, but we never know their innermost thoughts. How often do we discover to our surprise that a neighbour or a relative was dogged by years of depression, guilt and suffering?

Negative thoughts are like rats. They arrive in groups. One shows up, and before you know it they have taken over.

EXAMPLE: You take a phone call from a rude customer at work. Your first thought is: *"I hate rude people."*

ANDREW MATTHEWS

Followed by your next negative thought: "In this job *I'm surrounded by rude people!"*

And your next negative thought: "In this job I'm surrounded by rude people *and I'm underpaid."*

And the next: "In this job I'm surrounded by rude people and I'm underpaid *and under-appreciated."*

And then: "In this job I'm surrounded by rude people and I'm underpaid and under-appreciated *and come to think of it, I'm not appreciated by my husband, either."*

Now the rats are arriving in droves: "In this job I'm surrounded by rude people and I'm underpaid and under-appreciated and I'm not appreciated by my husband *and tonight I'll have to cook dinner. Why can't he get off his backside? My mother always told me I was making a serious mistake. And now I've got a headache. Maybe it's a tumour!"*

Is this familiar? A lone rat becomes a plague.

You need an extermination strategy, and here is the best strategy I know to rid yourself of the rats. The moment you have your first negative thought, you ask yourself, "What's good about this?"

What's good about confronting rude people?

- "I'm building character and patience."
- "I'm developing people skills that will help me in my next job."
- "The rude people at work help me to appreciate my husband."

Now you might say, "Let's be realistic." HERE'S REALISTIC:

- Lousy things happen.
- Happy people have the habit of saying, "What's good about this?"

You break your leg. "What's good about this?"

- "I get to rest."
- "I'll learn to empathise with sick people."
- "I'll read some great books."

Your girlfriend dumps you. "What's good about this?"

- "I can save money."
- "I'll see more of my buddies."
- "I can watch all the football I like."

In a Nutshell
One negative thought attracts another.
One positive thought attracts another.
Before the plague starts, ask yourself,
"What's good about this?"

"I tried being positive and it doesn't work!"

Fred has lived for twenty years on hamburgers, doughnuts and Coca Cola. He is overweight and exhausted.

Then he discovers a book that says, *"What you put in your mouth matters."* He buys some carrots and beans. He eats salad for four days.

After four days, Fred says, "I feel no better and I'm always hungry!" Fred goes back to burgers.

As almost anyone knows, four days of salad is a good start, but it can't reverse twenty years of junk!

It is the same with our thinking.

Mary has lived for twenty years with a head full of junk thoughts: "I am useless. I hate my life. I hate my job. I can never pay my bills."

She has the occasional happy thought, "I love my dog." But the rest of the time is mostly, "Life is tough and then you die."

Then she reads an inspirational book that says, *"What you think about, you become."* She tries to imagine herself as happy and successful. She tells herself, "I am abundant. I am a winner."

She sticks with the positive thinking for four days. (Her husband thinks that she has joined a weird cult.)

After four days she looks at her pile of unpaid bills, and says, "My life is no better." She gives up. "That was too hard and it's ridiculous."

Here's the point: you can't fix a lifetime of junk eating in a few days, and you can't fix a lifetime of junk thinking in a few days – or a few weeks.

Before we dismiss the idea that the quality of our thoughts creates our quality of life, we should ask ourselves, "Have I thoroughly tested this?"

In a Nutshell

What you think about, you become.
But many people give up too soon.

We might also ask the question,
"What is a thought?"

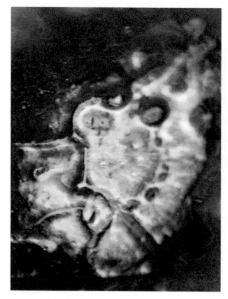

Polluted water from the
Fujiwara Dam.

The same water after a
prayer offering
by a Buddhist monk.

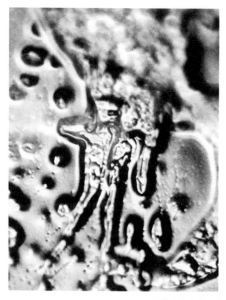

"You disgust me!"

"Love and gratitude."

What Is a Thought?

5

You might say, "If only someone could *demonstrate* that my thoughts create my reality, then I would be careful what I think. If someone could show that thought affects matter …"

Well, one Japanese researcher has been demonstrating it for years.

Dr Masaru Emoto has spent decades studying water. He freezes it and then photographs the ice crystals under a dark field microscope. Now, here's what's fascinating: he talks to the water before he freezes it, and the ice crystals respond to his conversation.

To one jar of water he'll say, *"I love you,"* and to another jar he'll say, *"You're ugly."* The water that is *appreciated* forms exquisite, highly organised crystals – like jewels. And the water that is criticised crystallises into ugly blobs.

Already, this sounds like science fiction, but it gets more amazing. Dr Emoto has demonstrated that you don't even have to *talk* to the water to influence the crystals. You can just think a word –

Here is hard evidence that your thoughts affect the world around you.

and send that thought to the water – and the ice crystals will reflect the quality of your thoughts.

And it gets more crazy. You don't even have to *send a thought.* You can simply write a word on the side of the jar, freeze the water and observe similar results. Words of love, encouragement and gratitude produce breathtaking crystals. Words of hate and criticism produce very different formations.

Emoto has experimented with writing all kinds of words on the jars: *gratitude, hope, hate, home cooking, convenience food.* He uses different languages and gets the same results. He plays music – Beethoven, Mozart and heavy metal – to water and photographs the crystals. The illustrations opposite are selected from hundreds in his books and from his website, www.masaru-emoto.net.[5]

Dr Emoto has shared his research at the United Nations. His books are in over forty languages. His findings are a stunning illustration of how our world works. Here is hard evidence that your thoughts affect the world around you.

Emoto's work is supported by other research. McGill University Associate Professor, Bernard Grad,[6] who examined water after it had been "treated" by people with healing abilities, discovered that there was *"a fundamental change in the bonding of the hydrogen and oxygen in its molecular makeup."* Russian research[7] supports Grad's findings.

We could list any number of experiments with similar findings, involving people in steel boxes, psychic plants and baby rabbits in submarines. Even Albert Einstein conducted his own experiments to explore the phenomenon of remote communication. He coined the term, "Spooky Action at a Distance".

ANDREW MATTHEW

The Old Reality

You ask, "So what does science have to say about the work of Drs Emoto and Grad?" Mostly, it pretends these things don't happen!

Here's the problem: modern science stands on the foundation of history's greatest scientist, Sir Isaac Newton. Newton formulated the laws of motion and gravitation, and advanced our understanding of mathematics, mechanics, astronomy and more.

He also conducted many experiments to demonstrate the influence of mind on matter.

But some of his work was lost in a laboratory fire, and some of it has been misunderstood. Modern science has totally ignored Newton's conclusions on the nature of thought.

Science has used *a mere portion* of Newton's life work to conclude that the Universe operates like a giant machine. This view of the Cosmos is known as the "Newtonian Model", and we stuck with it for 400 years.

You learned it at school: your teachers showed you diagrams of atoms and told you a) atoms are the building blocks of everything, b) everything can be measured and c) thought has no effect on the physical world.

But Newton was a student of ancient wisdom. The idea of a *mechanical Universe unaffected by prayer or human thought* – that we attribute to Newton – is a very convenient model, but NEWTON WOULD NOT AGREE WITH IT! And this model can't explain Dr Emoto's crystals.

We now know that some things cannot be measured and that the Universe is not like a machine.

The New Reality

We now have microscopes that allow us *to see inside atoms* and we have received some big surprises. We discovered that:

- solid little atoms are *not really solid.* They are, in fact, packets of energy
- these packets of energy *appear and disappear*
- a single particle can be in two different places at once. That's right! The exact same molecule can be in your kitchen and in your bedroom at precisely the same instant.

This is the world of quantum physics. There is no such thing as solid matter. As astrophysicist, Sir Arthur Eddington, said, "The stuff of the world is mind-stuff." [8]

So what does this all mean?

If you are battling to pay bills or fighting chicken pox, the physical world seems fairly real! Almost anybody would suggest that parking tickets and viruses are *real things,* and thoughts and feelings are *less real.*

So why would anyone argue that our thoughts can affect things?

Because the Universe is not like a big machine; it is much more like a big thought. But here's what's extraordinary: people talk about quantum physics in science class or at a dinner party, but beyond that, they mostly pretend it never happened.

The crazy New Age idea that everything is *consciousness* turns out to be cutting-edge science! You are consciousness, everything around you is consciousness, and how you think and feel determines what you get.

You might say, "Okay, so everything we know is made of thought energy. BUT my thoughts are just one small collection of energy in this humungous soup of thoughts we call the Cosmos. How could *my thoughts* possibly be interacting with *all that is* to create my life experience?"

The Universe is an energy system, constantly bringing itself into balance. You are part of it.

Every time you have a thought – "I want a new job", "I might get the 'flu", "I never have enough money", "Everything will work out fine" – you shift the balance. The balance restores itself as your thoughts materialise.

In a Nutshell
Thoughts are real things. Thoughts change situations.

From Nothing?
Be Logical!
You say, "But wait! How can solid stuff materialise from the invisible?"

Well, let's look at how the Universe got here in the first place. Most people believe in one of three possibilities:

1. God made the Universe from nothing, and we don't know how
2. The Universe exploded from nothing – The Big Bang theory
3. The Big Bang theory was God's idea – in other words, a big bang is a very cost-effective way for God to make a Universe.

You say, "Out of nothing? Let's be logical."

Well, scientists are logical. So what does Professor Stephen Hawking, the world's most celebrated cosmologist, have to say about creating solid stuff from nothing? He says:

> **But without a doubt, the most remarkable fact of all, is that the entire, enormous universe, all the innumerable galaxies, even time and space and the forces of nature themselves, simply materialized out of nothing.**[9]

Solid stuff appearing from nothing has a long history.

He says that everything erupted from the void as a boiling furnace of hydrogen. Eventually, this pure energy cooled into countless sub-atomic particles and became the Universe you know – including our Earth and Moon, the Himalayas, your eyelashes, the gold on your finger, a hundred billion other galaxies and all the chocolate in Belgium – out of nothing.

Scientists say the Universe came from nothing. Spiritual people say God made the Universe from nothing. *Visible* appearing from the *invisible* has a long history.

You say, "But that's not logical!"

Nothing about the Cosmos is logical. Nothing about life itself is logical.

We live in an ever-expanding Universe. How logical is that? And what is the Universe expanding into? Space that is already there? Or space that isn't there?

And what is at the edge of the Universe? A fence?

In a Nutshell
The Universe isn't logical.
It is magical.

You Get What You Feel

6

Thought and feelings have their own magnetic energy which attracts energy of a similar nature … This is the principle that whatever you put into the Universe will be reflected back to you.

"What this means from a practical standpoint is that we always attract into our lives whatever we think about most, believe in most strongly, expect on the deepest levels and/or imagine most vividly.[10]

Shakti Gawain

I was sitting on a plane waiting to depart Hobart airport. We were delayed by one final, rather breathless and angry-looking passenger.

While you are feeling bad, life jumps on your head.

When she saw that some guy had parked his big, black, heavy briefcase in the spot above her seat, she became angrier. When she discovered that there was no room for her bags anywhere in the overhead lockers, she began to look seriously disturbed.

And so she sat seething for the entire flight with her bag wedged between her feet, irritated by the offending briefcase.

You might guess the story from here. We landed; the owner of the briefcase stood up, reached over to retrieve it from the locker and dropped it on her head.

BAM! When you FEEL that life is against you, it is.

We attract people and circumstances that match how we feel. When we feel happy, we attract positive circumstances, and when we feel upset and angry, we attract events to make us feel worse.

The Rules of the Game

Imagine that you were playing a ball game and you didn't know the rules – and other players kept jumping on your head.

Wouldn't you feel like a victim? Wouldn't you decide, "This is unfair! I don't want to play anymore!"?

But then if someone explained the rules – "While you are holding the ball anyone can jump on your head" – that would really help!

The game of life is similar. You need to know the rules, which are: WHILE YOU ARE FEELING BAD, LIFE JUMPS ON YOUR HEAD. Whenever you are radiating thoughts such as *"I'm hopeless, angry, frustrated, jealous, scared, a victim"*, life beats you up.

No wonder some people decide, "Life is unfair! I don't want to play anymore!"

When you are happy, life and people reward you in the most unexpected ways. When you are stressed, angry, or feeling like a victim, life kicks you in the teeth.

When is it that you jam your finger, bite your tongue, stub your toe? Does it happen on days when you are feeling great? No, it happens when you are frustrated and angry with yourself.

When do airlines lose your baggage? On those days when you are happy and excited? Or at the end of a long trip when you are exhausted and coming down with the 'flu?

ANDREW MATTHEWS

What comes first? Thoughts? Or feelings?

Most often, it seems, thoughts create feelings, a bit like ingredients create a cake.

● You take a thought, *"My husband always leaves his empty beer cans on the coffee table"*, blend it with *"He never even noticed my new haircut"* and let it stew overnight with *"I can't sleep because of his constant snoring"* and you create an angry feeling.

- You take a thought, *"I'm lucky to have a job"*, mix it with *"Most days are good days"* and sprinkle it with *"Life is getting better"* and you create a happy feeling.

The THOUGHTS in your head become A FEELING in your heart.

Here's the good news: changing your thoughts can change how you feel.

Negative Thoughts

Here's more good news: a few negative thoughts won't ruin your life.

You have up to 50,000 thoughts per day. Amongst those 50,000 thoughts, some are bound to be a bit negative.

The odd passing thought won't make you rich or poor, happy or miserable.

But a whole bunch of thoughts is a different matter.

Lots of similar thoughts – for example, lots of happy thoughts or lots of *"Life is lousy"* thoughts – become a feeling that you may hold onto for a whole day or a week or a lifetime.

We Attract What We Feel

One morning in 2004, my wife, Julie, and I had a disagreement. I said something insensitive that made her furious. I don't remember what I said, but in twenty years I had never seen her so mad.

As Julie grabbed her car keys and left for her appointment I thought to myself, "No one who is as angry as Julie is right now should be anywhere near an automobile!"

Not ten minutes later, she was sitting in her car at an intersection, perfectly stationary. A van approached the crossroads at high speed, lost control – and drove straight into Julie's car. Thank God she escaped unhurt.

As Julie soon discovered, the van was driven by another very angry lady.

You ask:

- Was Julie thinking about a car accident? No!
- Did Julie want the accident? No!
- Was she experiencing intense negative emotion? Yes!
- Did she have an intensely negative experience
  to match her feelings? Absolutely!

You say, "But Julie's car wasn't even moving. It wasn't her fault!"

Ask Julie and she will admit that she created her experience. She will tell you that she had a head full of *"Today is lousy"* thoughts, and life delivered an experience to match. You are a magnet. How you feel about yourself determines the quality of your experience.

You say, "Does that mean that everyone who is angry in a car will have an accident?" No. It means that if you are full of an energy that says, *"Life stinks"*, then life will deliver you *"Life stinks"* experiences. And if you are driving a car at the time, an accident is more likely.

If you are having intense feelings of stress – you feel that life is unfair, that you are being punished by people who are irresponsible – then life will deliver you an experience that will match that feeling. It might be an accident, it might be an illness, or it might be something else unpleasant.

Uplifting thoughts attract uplifting experiences. Angry, victim-type thoughts attract low-energy experiences. You can't determine the exact nature of all your experiences by how you feel – who you meet and exactly what happens – but you determine the QUALITY of your experiences.

In a Nutshell

When you are feeling angry or depressed and you ask yourself, "What else can go wrong?" the answer is, "Quite a lot!"

A Magical Life

> **A change of feeling is a change of destiny.**[11]
> **Neville Goddard**

Did this ever happen to you?

- You went to an inspiring seminar
- You read an uplifting book
- You joined a church
- You fell in love.

You felt so good. Life was different, almost magical. It was like you had begun a whole new chapter. You were optimistic. Challenges were easier to handle, you had more energy, and people were nicer. Maybe you thought, "This is the how my life will be from now on."

You were cruising – for three weeks. Then gradually, things returned to normal.

So what happened? Were you kidding yourself? Were you deluded?

No, you weren't. You were simply FEELING better, and your happier feelings created happier circumstances. But then your energy dropped – maybe you suffered a disappointment or two – and you were back to normal.

But some people never return to the *old normal*. They begin a new chapter in their life and create a *new normal*.

- They keep reading inspirational books
- They mix with uplifting people
- They develop immovable faith
- They fall deeper in love.

In other words, they keep FEELING good. And so they become one of those people who live a charmed life, who turn defeat into victory and who always meet the right people at the right time.

In a Nutshell

It's not *what you know* so much as how you feel.

Get the Feeling

To get what you want, you first need to have the feeling of what you want – as if it has already arrived. You may ask, "Isn't that the same as prayer?"

It can be, but it usually isn't.

Most of us learned to pray in a different way, such as: *"God, I am a powerless sinner and my life is a mess. Can you please fix it?"* This approach doesn't work, and now we know why. If you are filled with feelings of disappointment and powerlessness, and the belief that *"I am a bad person"*, you create more experiences to match.

Lost in Translation

So you ask, "If the most powerful form of prayer is to feel the feeling of your wish fulfilled, why isn't that spelled out in Christian teachings?"

It was. But it got watered down and lost in translation. For example, in the modern condensed King James Bible, in John 16:24, we read: "Ask and ye shall receive that your joy may be full."

So what is lost?

Compare this with the original text: "Ask without hidden motive and be surrounded by your answer. BE ENVELOPED BY WHAT YOU DESIRE, that your gladness may be full."[12] In other words, feel it all around you, already complete.

Traditional cultures the world over acknowledge the power of feeling. The Navajo Indians understand that you don't *wish* for rain. You FEEL the rain. You give thanks that it has already arrived.

Tibetan Buddhist Monks know that the most powerful form of prayer is to pray FEELING THAT THE PRAYER HAS BEEN ANSWERED.

In his book, *Secrets of the Lost Mode of Prayer*, Gregg Braden[13] describes his experience in the mountains of Tibet. Braden wanted to know, "What is happening when monks pray?" What is happening when they chant? Why the gongs, the bells, the mantras? In a freezing stone monastery at 14,000 feet, Braden asks the abbot, "When we see your prayers, what are you doing ... what is happening on the inside?"

The monk replies, "What you have seen is what we do to create the feeling in our bodies. *Feeling is the prayer!*"

Feeling is the prayer. That is how life works.

Why is it that Muslims, Hindus, Buddhists Christians and Jews – whether they be fundamentalist, orthodox, unorthodox, charismatic, neo-charismatic or metrosexual – believe in prayer? It is because it is not about your particular *brand* or *religious faction,* and it is not about the *words*. It is about the feeling.

When your feeling is a perfect match with your goal – or to put it another way, when all doubt is eliminated – the goal is yours.

At times in my life I thought, "If I just suffer enough, maybe God – if He is up there – will feel sorry for me. Maybe He'll send me a million dollars."

It didn't happen.

Mostly, it seemed, the guys who received a million were the guys who already had a million: *"For to one who has it, it will be given and it will be increased."*[14]

Affirmations

Affirmations are positive phrases that we repeat to ourselves over and over. You have probably heard of phrases like *"I am a money magnet"* or *"Every day in every way I'm getting better and better and better."*

Some people swear by them. Other people swear that they are a waste of energy. How can this be?

It is because it is not the words that matter; it's the feeling. Affirmations without feeling ARE useless; you may as well chant phone numbers.

But if you can feel your affirmations, if you regularly tell yourself things like, "I have everything I need", "My life is getting better", "I am loved and I am loveable", "I am healthy", "I am rich", and feel it and believe it, life will get better.

First Get the Feeling

We grow up believing, "When things get better, THEN I will feel better." It sounds reasonable. But it is the slow way to get results, and it is hard work.

> "Just when I thought I had found Mr Right he became Mr Learning Experience."

- Try fixing a relationship while you feel bad about it
- Try getting rich when you feel poor
- Try succeeding in a job you hate.

When is it that you start to climb out of any mess? Only when you start to feel hopeful.

FIRST comes a glimmer of hope. Then, perhaps you get some encouragement from a friend. You start to feel better. You read a book. You take a long walk. You feel better still. You get a little inspiration. Other people arrive to help. You are on your way.

But first, you need that glimmer of hope, a little belief. Only THEN do things start to improve. It all happens AFTER you begin to feel better.

In a Nutshell

Experience follows feeling. Feeling is the prayer.

Finding Mr Right

What do many people do when they are looking for love? They hang out in sleazy bars drinking more than they want. The results are often disappointing. Explains Mary, "Just when I thought I had found *Mr Right,* he became *Mr Learning Experience!"*

You don't have to trawl the bars and you don't have to impress anybody.

People in happy relationships will tell you, "I always knew there would be someone for me." They felt it.

Your mission is to FEEL loved – not WISHING you had it but FEELING YOU HAVE IT now – by imagining your perfect relationship and by being kind to yourself.

When you start with the feeling, the Universe will begin to organise itself around you. Opportunities will arise. You go with the flow.

When you finally have that "knowing" that he is out there and when you stop being in a hurry for him to arrive, Mr Right will walk into your life. No one can keep him out.

In a Nutshell
If you want to see it happen you first need to feel it happen.

Relax!
In the 1980s I taught a weekend relaxation course. Over two and half days, the attendees also learned to like themselves a little more.

Here's what amazed me: in the weeks following their course, people would report all kinds of wonderful happenings. "My back pain has disappeared!" "My boss is friendlier." "I just got promoted." "My family is more considerate." "My husband is more loving." "I slashed my golf handicap!"

So I would ask them, "What did you visualise to make this happen?" So often they would say, "Nothing."

Year in, year out, the story was the same for most of the attendees. I wondered, "Why are all these people reporting such positive results? All they learned to do was relax and feel better!"

You are a complex ball of energy. Your energy ball includes every thought, wish and fear you have ever had. Your energy is creating your life, moment by moment. You don't have to figure everything out – but you do have to stop fighting and worrying and relax.

In a Nutshell
When we feel better, better things happen.

"What if I Can't Feel Better?"

You say, "How can I feel great when I feel terrible?"
You can't. You don't have to. You just take one
step at a time.

If we were to rank emotions on a ladder,
with the most positive at the top, we might
list them like so:

10. Love and Joy
9. Happiness
8. Optimism
7. Contentment
6. Pessimism
5. Disappointment
4. Worry
3. Anger
2. Hatred and Revenge
1. Fear and Grief

So you ask, "How do I get from fear to joy?" The same way you get from first
gear to tenth gear on a bicycle, or from first gear to fifth gear in your car. You just
move to the next gear.

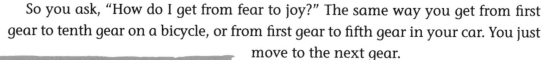

If you can feel a little better today and a little better tomorrow, that's enough.

You don't jump from hatred to joy
overnight – but you can move from hatred
to anger. And anger feels better than
hatred. That's progress.

It's how life works – one step at a time,
one rung at a time. You don't go from $30,000 per year to $300,000 per year,
but you can get to $40,000 and then $60,000 and keep going. It is like building
muscle, getting healthy or learning a new language.

If you can feel a little better today and a little better tomorrow, that's enough.

It Doesn't Seem Fair

You say, "What if I am ill or in pain? How do you expect me to feel happy and
positive? It's not fair!"

Maybe it isn't fair — but it is a law of life: *for your circumstances to improve, you first have to feel more positive.*

Laws don't care what you think. It's like with gravity: if you trip over the cat and break your arm, you can argue, "Gravity isn't fair!" But gravity doesn't care.

It might seem like a cruel twist: "Why should I have to FEEL successful or loved before I can BE successful or loved?" It may seem like an odd way to run a Universe. But here is how the spiritual masters explain it:

You are a part of everything. No one is stopping you from having anything. God is not stopping you from having anything. You already have everything you want; you just don't know it. The only thing in your way is YOUR BELIEFS.

When you change your beliefs – and as everything is vibration, this means when you change your vibration – your goals begin to drop in your lap.

In a Nutshell

Life doesn't happen *to* you. Life happens *through* you.

The Eleventh Hour

Have you noticed that things usually look most bleak just before they start to get better? The entrepreneur is down to his last dollar when he finally scores the big deal. The injured athlete is ready to quit, but she gives it one last shot and wins the gold medal.

You see it all the time in movies. You see it in movies because it happens all the time in life. There is a principle at work here. The darkest hour is often just before the dawn. It is almost like life tests us: "Are you serious?"

The bigger the goal, the darker it gets.

In a Nutshell

This darkness before the dawn is known as *the eleventh hour*. But the eleventh hour is an impostor. So often, if we just hang on, the tide will turn.

The Law of Attraction

7

Your mind is like an iceberg: the power is in the part that you don't see. Every thought and feeling that you have ever had is there in your subconscious. It is driving your life.

So the question is, "How do I program my subconscious to create and attract what I want?"

The answer that few people know – and the reason for this book – is that FEELINGS reprogram your subconscious. Neville Goddard, 20th century lecturer and author, explains in his book, *Feeling Is the Secret*:

> **Ideas are impressed on the subconscious through the medium of feeling. No idea can be expressed on the subconscious mind until it is felt … The subconscious is the womb of creation … It never changes the idea received but always gives it form.**[15]

You impress your subconscious by FEELING what you want to be; you have to feel rich, feel successful, and feel loved FIRST. To get it, you have to feel it.

Whatever changes you want to make in your life, you have to feel them. As Gandhi said, "We must be the change we want to see."

In a Nutshell

Everything starts within. Buddha summed it up 2600 years ago: "You are not of this world; this world is in you."

Everything Has a Unique Vibration

You say, "That's fine for Buddha, but I want a logical scientific explanation! How do MY thoughts and feelings attract things?"

Let's take a closer look at vibration.

Even to cavemen, it was obvious that SOUND is actually vibration. Then, in the 17th century we began to understand that LIGHT is actually vibration.

And in the 20th century – after scientists broke atoms into smaller and smaller particles – we finally realised that MATTER is actually vibration. Everything is vibration! And of course, vibration is energy.

A peanut is a peanut only because its energy has a particular vibration or frequency. So, too, for a diamond, a feather or a French fry.

For the *Law of Attraction* to work – or even for us to consider it seriously – every bit of matter in the Universe would need to have a *different frequency* from every other bit.

Every peanut would need to vibrate differently from every other peanut. Every sparrow, bacterium, lottery ticket and Lamborghini would need a unique signature or "cosmic bar code", so that it can be found in this warehouse we call the Universe.

NOTE: *If you are not so interested in science, you may choose to skim over the next few paragraphs and re-join me at "Chain Reactions".*

A unique vibration for everything in the Universe! Is this possible?

According to quantum physics and Professor Wolfgang Pauli, absolutely! Wolfgang Pauli won a Nobel Prize – and Albert Einstein's admiration – for his part in discovering a new law of nature, now known as the *Pauli Exclusion Principle.*[16]

In physics we learn that all electrons have three properties: a) energy level, b) spin and c) orbit. Physicists multiply the energy level, spin and orbit to calculate the "quantum number" of an electron.

Pauli discovered that NO TWO ELECTRONS IN THE UNIVERSE CAN HAVE THE SAME NUMBER!

So What?

To examine this law, let's take an apple – and from the billions of electrons within the apple, let's choose just one electron. We'll call him Eric the Electron. Eric's quantum number would be an impossibly long one, but to keep things simple, let's pretend his quantum number is 23.

Pauli proved that nowhere in the Universe – not in all the apples in all the world, not in some distant shooting star, not even in the whisker of an arctic mouse – can there be another electron with the quantum number 23.

It's a bit like every electron in the Universe belonging to the same football team, and no two electrons being allowed to have the same number!

So what happens if we polish the apple? Friction adds energy. Energy increases Eric's quantum number. Suddenly, Eric's quantum number jumps to, say, 26.

At the exact instant that Eric's number leaps to 26, the one electron in the entire Universe with a quantum number of 26 – whether it is out beyond the Milky Way or in your porridge – will instantly change.

Chain Reactions

When you polish an apple, when you kiss your lover, when you curse your neighbour, when you forgive your brother, when you scratch your backside, you send chain reactions across the Universe. Each time one of Earth's seven billion people has a fleeting thought, electrons across the Universe adjust. Each time you have a thought, electrons across the Cosmos adjust.

Our Universe is rearranging itself every millisecond, bringing itself into balance. Professor Pauli proved it – and it is not even cutting-edge science. Pauli won his Nobel Prize in 1945.

We are not lone cogs in some giant machine. We are wrapped in one giant living, breathing blanket. Some call it consciousness.

If every electron has a unique vibration, then every thing has a unique vibration. Science confirms the teachings of Buddha, Aristotle and Jesus Christ:

- Everything in the Universe is connected
- Thought doesn't just affect matter; thought is matter.

This Is Nothing New

Here's the good news. Whatever you have in your life right now, you created. With your vibration, you attracted it. This means that when you change how you feel, you change what shows up.

You say, "How do we change our vibes?" When we find a way to:

- look for good things every day
- quit blaming everyone else
- quit blaming ourselves
- quit worrying
- see the best in people.

You may notice something. This is what great spiritual teachers have always taught: BE GRATEFUL, FORGIVE PEOPLE, LOVE MORE, BLAME LESS AND BELIEVE THINGS WILL WORK OUT! This is how you become a magnet for everything you want.

In a Nutshell

All that spiritual advice we heard over the years – that seemed like it was designed to punish us – actually makes us more powerful.

"What do sensible people say?"

You may say, "This idea that *'We are all connected and our thoughts create our reality'* sounds very New Age.

"What do *practical people* say about this? What do serious business people say?"

Let's start with the industrialist, Andrew Carnegie. He used his understanding of the subconscious mind to become the richest man in the world.

Ultimately, Carnegie decided to share his success strategies. So he commissioned the young journalist, Napoleon Hill, to work alongside him and write a book to explain his secrets.

Carnegie introduced Hill to dozens of entrepreneurs, including Henry Ford. Ford *also* understood the subconscious mind and became one of the world's richest men.

Hill's book, *The Law of Success in 16 Lessons,* ultimately became *Think and Grow Rich,*[17] and remains an international best-seller eighty years later. The central message of *Think and Grow Rich* is:

● WHAT THE MIND OF MAN CAN CONCEIVE AND BELIEVE, IT CAN ACHIEVE
● YOU BECOME WHAT YOU THINK ABOUT MOST OF THE TIME.

Nevertheless, most of the millions of people that read the book never achieved all their dreams. There are some concepts in *Think and Grow Rich* that deserve further explanation, for example, "What's happening when the law of attraction seems broken?"

When the Law of Attraction Fails

8

Janice wrote:

Dear Andrew

I knew about the Law of Attraction long before it became popular in New Age books. I would picture myself working in a new company, and somehow it would happen, almost by magic and without effort. I would see myself living in an imaginary apartment and then find that apartment by accident.

I would imagine parking spaces in impossible places and get them. If I wanted to read a book or watch a video, I would see it in my mind, and a stranger would miraculously give it to me, or I would find it in a second-hand store when I was looking for furniture.

I also attracted some bad stuff when I worried too much about what I didn't want!

The key always seemed to be: be happy, and relax into the knowing that it will happen. It is how I have mostly lived my life. I have also often wished I had a million dollars, but it never landed in my lap.

In your book, Follow Your Heart, you talked about attracting things. So here's my question: why is it that I can attract so many things that I want but not the million dollars?

Is there a limit to this stuff? Why is it that this Law of Attraction doesn't always work? Could it be that that God says, "No!"?

Janice

> *"Why is it that I can attract so many things I want but not the million dollars?"*

Here's what has taken me thirty years to figure out, and what *most books* don't thoroughly explain.

When the Law of Attraction *seems* to be broken, it's usually because:

- we chose a goal that didn't really excite us
- we got stuck in "reverse gear" – meaning we focused on LACK
- we chose goals we didn't really believe were possible.

Let's examine these points one at a time – and look at what to do about it.

Choose a Goal You Really Want

Excitement makes things happen fast. It's the E-MOTION that sets your dreams in motion.

Feelings of disappointment, jealousy, boredom or desperation slow life to a crawl. That's why it helps to be enthusiastic about our life and our plans.

Sometimes, we choose a goal that we think is exciting, but it's not. If the goal is not exciting, we don't keep thinking about it; so we don't attract it.

The perfect example is a million dollars.

Anyone might argue that a million dollars is really exciting, but actually it's boring. It's just a bunch of paper. Would you ever spend your time dreaming about a boxful of cash? You wouldn't. A million dollars sitting in the bank might seem like a nice idea, but it will never give you butterflies in your stomach.

What is exciting is WHAT YOU CAN DO with a million dollars: you can create a new business, take your kids to Disneyland, shift house, buy your son a mountain bike, enjoy a world cruise, quit your job and go study archaeology.

People who succeed don't dream about money. They dream about *how they will make it* and *what they will do with it*. They feel it in their bones.

You need to feel yourself experiencing your goals. Photographs on your refrigerator help. Pictures of Alaskan cruise ships or your dream apartment keep you excited. Photographs on your wall, bathroom mirror, phone or screensaver of the special dog, horse, car, boat, helicopter, bicycle or guitar that you want to own, keep you on-track.

Focus on What You Want

Now here is where many people – like Fred – get confused.

Fred says, "I've been thinking about my dream for twenty years, and it never happened!"

But most likely, Fred has been thinking about NOT having his dream. He's been upset and disappointed about missing out for twenty years, and you can't attract anything good when you are angry, upset or disappointed.

Here's a little example of how we sometimes shift our attention from HAVING something to NOT HAVING something. Imagine that you walk into Joe's Restaurant in your lunch hour.

- You order your favourite pizza.
- Fifteen minutes go by and no pizza. ("Where's my lunch?" Already you are annoyed.)
- The ladies at the next table get their spaghetti marinara. ("What? I was here first!" Now you are angry!)
- You complain to the waiter, "Where is my pizza?"
- You text your friend, "They forgot my pizza!"
- Forty-five minutes go by and no pizza. The ladies finish their coffees and leave. You are furious. You grab your coat and storm out.

So what were you thinking about while you were waiting? You say, "I was thinking about my pizza!" But you weren't. You were thinking about your pizza for the first fifteen minutes. After that, it was all *LACK of pizza*.

For your subconscious mind, PIZZA and LACK of PIZZA are two totally different subjects. PIZZA IS ON ITS WAY has a light, happy vibration, and THEY FORGOT MY PIZZA is a heavy, angry vibration!

So often, we think that we are dwelling on *what we want* and we expect the Law of Attraction to *deliver,* but we are actually pumping out the "I HAVE NO PIZZA" vibration. So we keep *moving away from what we want.*

MATTHEWS

So what are some typical LACK thoughts?

- I wish I was rich
- I wish I was confident
- I wish I had a different job
- I wish I had a loving, caring husband
- I wish I was healthy
- Where's my damn pizza?

How do you know these are LACK statements? Because when you repeat any of them you feel bad. And when you feel bad you get more lack.

Stuck in Reverse Gear

Fred says, "I think about money all the time, but I am broke."

Actually, Fred is thinking about NOT HAVING money all the time. Thinking about the LACK of prosperity is the exact opposite to thinking about prosperity. Fred is stuck in reverse gear and doesn't know it.

You say, "Does it matter?" It matters! It matters more than people ever imagine.

Feast or Famine

How often do you hear this?

Bill applies for twenty jobs in twelve months without luck. As soon as he gets hired, he gets three more job offers. Why? He spent a year focused on lack. As soon as he got a job, his energy shifted from lack – "*Nobody wants me*" – to "*People want me.*" When you feel wanted, people hire you. Bingo!

Or this? A couple try for ten years to have a baby. Eventually they adopt – and immediately she gets pregnant! They went ten years with the feeling of *no baby*. When suddenly they had the joy and the feeling of having a child – baby!

So How Do I Know if My Thinking Is Creating Good Results?

It is so simple, it is ridiculous. If you feel GOOD when you are thinking about your goal, you are creating good things. If you feel BAD when you are thinking about your goal, you are creating what you don't want.

You impress your subconscious by how you FEEL – nothing else. Your mission is to FEEL GOOD EVERY WAKING HOUR. Your mission is to feel good every time you think about what you want.

Fred says, "How can you think about a million dollars and feel bad?" Very easily. Most people do.

In a Nutshell

When you feel good, you are creating what you want.
When you feel bad, you are creating what you don't want.

Luke Skywalker: "I can't believe it."
Yoda: "That is why you fail."[18]

You Need to Believe It Is Possible

Fred reads one of those books that says, "You can have, be or do anything you want." Fred sets his first goal: a multi-million-dollar mansion. He thinks about it once or twice.

When he thinks about it he feels bad because a) he really doesn't believe he'll get it, and b) he's thinking about those snooty, rich people in nice houses. Fred soon gives up on the mansion.

Day by day you notice, "Life works when I am feeling good."

You ask, "To get something, do you need to believe it is possible?" Yes, you do.

If you believe your goal is possible you feel good thinking about it. Because you feel good thinking about it, you often think about it. You are comfortable with it.

We achieve goals with which we are totally comfortable.

How important is belief? The entertainer, Seal, shares his experience:

> **It wasn't that we were the best at what we do. Where we grew up there were people who sang way better than we could – but no one believed harder than we did, and that belief was unrelenting.**[19]

Unrelenting belief. You just keep on pumping out that vibration.

Why Belief Matters

Let's say you want to get fit, you want a better job or you want a happier relationship with your husband. If you believe it is perfectly possible, you enjoy thinking about it every spare moment. So believing it and feeling good cause it to happen.

But what if you don't believe it is possible? You feel bad thinking about it. So you don't think about it. So you don't attract it. You say, "HOW can I feel good? How can I believe in anything good when my life has been so disappointing?"

Small Steps

You develop your subconscious muscle like you develop any other muscle. You practise with everyday things. You practise feeling good with everything you do, every day. You set small goals, every day. Step by step. For example:

- You need to make a speech. You practise FEELING good about it. Ahead of time, you imagine yourself receiving congratulations from the entire crowd. You play mental movies of your own success.

- You are about to drive your car through an unfamiliar city in rush hour and you are feeling nervous. You imagine yourself in your car, RELAXED and singing to yourself.
- You are worried about paying your bills. You begin to visualise paying those bills with a smile on your face. You regularly affirm to yourself, "I have more money than I need!" More and more often you find yourself making ends meet with less and less stress.

Day by day, you notice that *"Life works when I'm feeling good."* People respond positively, opportunities evolve from the strangest "coincidences" and impossible problems evaporate.

Week by week, you develop a knowing that life is somehow arranging itself to suit you. You develop a quiet confidence that *"My life always works out."*

Your friends say "How?"

You say, "I don't know how. I don't even worry about how."

Now you have the muscle to manage bigger goals.

The books tell you, "Your mind is a magnet. Go out and have, be or do anything you want." Theoretically, it's true. But you need to build your subconscious muscle. You need to refine your ball of energy.

But HOW Does This All Happen?

The obvious questions are:

- How can I pay off my bills if I don't even know how to make the money?
- How can I sell my house in a bad market?
- How can I possibly get a better job?
- How will I meet my perfect mate?

It's a bit like the satellite saying, "How will my signal find the television?" It's not an issue. The signal is everywhere, but it only resonates with televisions that are tuned in.

When you assume the feeling of having found the perfect mate or job, your signal is everywhere – but you only attract the mate or boss who is vibrating at a similar frequency.

Successful entrepreneurs, authors, sports stars and happily married couples assume the feeling.

You don't have to always be in control. You don't even have to know HOW.

In a Nutshell
Your problem is not to figure out how. Your mission is just to assume the feeling.

Imagine!

9

In 1986 I decided to write a book. I knew nothing about writing books. Since school I had never written anything longer than a postcard. All I knew was that I had a title – *Being Happy!* – and I wanted to sell a million copies.

I wrote one page per day, before breakfast.

I also made a cassette recording to play in my car. It had a simple message that repeated over and over: *"'Being Happy!' is an international best-seller."* It continued for half an hour.

For the whole of 1987, I played this recording every time I got into my little red car. Well, actually, I only played it when I was alone – my friends seemed to prefer Dire Straits.

In mid-1987 I sent my completed *Being Happy!* manuscript to publishers around the world. All I received were rejections. The book may have been a success in my subconscious, but it wasn't doing very well anywhere else.

It seemed I had hit a brick wall.

Then in March 1988, I was passing through Singapore where I had lunch with a friend, Jacquie Seow. I asked her, "Would you like to read my manuscript?" Jacquie agreed to read it and said, "There is a publisher living in my apartment building. I'll show it to him."

I thought, "A Singaporean publisher? That's not part of my plan." I gave Jacquie the book but I didn't hold my breath.

Within two weeks, I had a publishing deal with Jacquie's neighbor, Ian, and within eighteen months I was living off my author's royalties. *Being Happy!*[1] continues to sell today.

You ask, "Andrew, what if you had never used the tape recording? Would it have happened anyway?"

Two Friends Play-acting

In the 1970s Fred Couples and Jim Nantz were buddies at the University of Houston. Fred was a dedicated golfer with dreams of winning the US Masters, and Jim had ambitions of becoming a top sports announcer.

Together, they would often play-act a scene where Fred, having just won the US Masters, was interviewed by the CBS announcer, Jim Nantz.

In 1992, Fred won the Masters. He was ushered into the Butler Cabin to receive the famous green jacket – and there, to get the inside story, was CBS's Jim Nantz.

At the close of the interview they embraced with tears in their eyes, no doubt reflecting on how the imaginary scene that they had so often rehearsed in Houston had just unfolded before the world in Augusta.

Would Fred Couples have won the Masters Golf Championship without the play-acting? Would Jim Nantz have achieved his dream without the play-acting? Would it all have happened anyway?

Here's what I know: there's not a successful actor, astronaut, brain surgeon, pilot, pop star, president or pole dancer who didn't imagine their dream over and over and over again long before it happened.

In a Nutshell

Everything is connected. Nothing happens "anyway".

What Happens When the Law of Attraction Doesn't Work?

Laws always work.

The law of gravity is never broken. For example, when a plane flies, it doesn't mean that the law of gravity is broken. It means that forces stronger than gravity are pulling the plane upward. Once there is enough momentum, the plane lifts off the ground.

The law of attraction is the same. You need momentum. You plant your goal firmly into your subconscious. Once it is there, you have it – but most importantly, IT HAS YOU.

When your goal has you, you don't have to figure everything out. It is more like you go along for the ride. When you have the *knowing* that you will be successful – and it is only a matter of WHEN – doing the work is a joy. Doing your best is automatic.

When your goal isn't showing up, one of these explanations is likely.

- You chose a boring goal and quit thinking about it; so you didn't attract it
- You got stuck in reverse gear with LACK thoughts. If you dwell on lack you get more lack
- You are doubting it, and when you doubt, you don't have the necessary FEELING to achieve your goal
- You never became comfortable with it.

"Set a Date!"

Here's something else that the books tell you, but which often doesn't help. They tell you, "Set a DATE!" They tell you, "Choose a date by which you will have bought the house, found the perfect wife, scored the dream job."

Dates usually add stress and give you reason to doubt.

Obviously, sometimes your plans are attached to a fixed date – a wedding, a speech or a tournament. It makes sense to see and feel those events unfolding perfectly, attached to a date. But in most other instances, see and feel your goals achieved and let them unfold in their own time.

So How Do I Know When My Goals Will Happen?

When your goal feels perfectly natural – when you say to yourself, "I know it is going to happen, and I am so comfortable that this will happen that I'm in no hurry" – that is when your dream job, or boyfriend, shows up.

But It Would Have Happened Anyway!

When life works out – when your lover walks into your life, when you get head-hunted by a rival company, when your headaches disappear, when your book hits the best-seller list – there's the question, "Did I attract this, or would it have happened anyway?"

When you feel good, and keep feeling good, opportunities and good people just keep on finding you. Just keep doing what works.

What about People Who Say, "This is all garbage!"?

I've always believed in magic. When I wasn't doing anything in this town, I'd go up every night, sit on Mulholland Drive, look out at the city, stretch out my arms and say, "Everybody wants to work with me. I'm a really good actor. I have all kinds of great movie offers."

I'd just repeat these things over and over, literally convincing myself that I had a couple of movies lined up. I'd drive down that hill, ready to take the world on, going, "Movie offers are out there for me. I just don't hear them yet." [2]

Jim Carrey, Actor

> *Some people just know that thoughts are magnetic. They don't need to be convinced.*

In 1990, comedian Jim Carrey was still struggling to get work. It was on one night during that year, sitting in his old Toyota looking down on Los Angeles, that he wrote himself a cheque. It was for ten million dollars, for acting services rendered.

Jim carried the cheque in his wallet. By 1995 he had starred in *Ace Ventura Pet Detective*, *The Mask* and *Dumb and Dumber*. His asking price was now twenty million dollars per movie.

Plenty of people don't believe that thought affects matter or that we create our own success. But here is a challenge for you: find one wildly successful person who doesn't believe it.

What do people like Jim Carrey, Oprah Winfrey (the first billion-dollar television host), Madonna (300 million albums sold) and Jack Canfield (500 million books in print) say about the power of the mind? They will tell you, "What you hold in your mind, you attract. What you hold in your mind, you become."

There are *other journalists* who interview as well as Oprah Winfrey. A million *other people* have had better ideas than Richard Branson.

But *the others* couldn't BELIEVE as well. And this includes your brother-in-law who says, "This is all fantasy!".

Who do you want to believe?

How Can I Be Happy When I Am Broke?

I was in a Kuala Lumpur shopping mall in 2013 when a man approached me. He was casually dressed but immaculate. He said, "Are you Andrew Matthews? I read your book twenty years ago."

I sensed he had a story to share. So I invited him to Starbucks.

He said, "I'm Teuku from Aceh in Indonesia. My family was very poor. When I was in university I was so poor that I owned just one pair of trousers. I was so poor that my girlfriend would give me *her* shirts to wear. Many days I had nothing to eat.

"When I was at my lowest point, a friend loaned me the Indonesian version of your book, *Being Happy!* [3]

"Apart from text books, it is the first book I ever read. I began to understand that we choose our thoughts. I began to focus on what I HAD instead of what I DIDN'T HAVE.

"I made a list on a card of everything I wanted for my future: a good job, a wife, two healthy children, an apartment, a nice car ..."

He leaned forward, "Today I am the regional business development manager for a multi-national corporation. I travel the world. I have a wife and two beautiful girls. They go to the best schools ..."

Teuku's eyes welled with tears. "Your book changed my life."

My eyes were full of tears, too. I felt so happy for Teuku.

I must make two points here. Firstly, my book didn't change his life; *Teuku changed his life*. Secondly, there is nothing new in my books. These principles have been around forever.

Teuku said, "I still have bad days. So I keep that card on my wall to remind me how far I have come."

He asked about my next book. I explained that *How Life Works* was about the power of emotion: "How you think matters, but the real power is in how you feel."

In a Nutshell

Teuku said, "For the last twenty years, whenever I wanted to get to the next step, I would try to feel what it would be like to be already there.

"When I was hungry I would try to feel what it would be like to have enough food. When I had no job I would try to feel what it is like to have a job. When I was a worker I would try to feel what it is like to be a manager."

He asked, "Is that what your book is about?"

Yes, Teuku, that is exactly, absolutely what this book is about!

What about those successful people who never read a book about the subconscious mind?

Some people just know that thoughts are magnetic. They don't need books. They don't need to be convinced.

Some people are born knowing what took me a thousand books and thirty years to understand. They just spend their life FEELING as good as they can and knowing that everything will work out.

They just know THIS IS HOW LIFE WORKS.

The World Is Your Mirror

10

ANDREW MATTHEWS

Have you noticed that when you leave the office feeling irate, people abuse you in the subway? The reverse is also true. How different the world looks when we fall in love!

The world is a mirror; what you feel inside, you get on the outside. This is why YOU CAN'T FIX LIFE BY WORKING ON THE OUTSIDE. If people on the street are unfriendly, changing streets doesn't help. If nobody at work gives you any respect, changing jobs won't fix it.

Most of us learned things inside out! We learned, "If you don't like your job, change it. If you don't like your wife, change her." Sometimes it's appropriate to change your job or your partner. But if you don't change your thinking, you are setting yourself up for more of the same.

EXAMPLE: Carol's husband Bob gives her no help. They both work nine to five, but Bob gives her no help with the kids and no help around the house. Weeknights he goes drinking; weekends he goes golfing. She feels like a servant and she resents him.

But it's not about Bob. It's about her. As long as she feels like a servant, she will be treated like a servant. For life to change, Carol has to value Carol. The minute she feels worthwhile, deserving and loveable, she will find support – either from Bob or from somebody else.

> *If you love yourself, people will love you.*

It's always about ourselves.

EXAMPLE: Friends and family are always imposing on you. Whenever somebody wants to shift house, they ask you to pack and carry boxes. When people need a ride to the airport at 4 am, they call you. You ask yourself, "Why don't they value MY time?"

Because you don't value your time! When you change, they change.

It's Not about THEM

Many people never get it. They spend a lifetime blaming other people – but it's not about OTHER PEOPLE.

- If you feel that you deserve to be paid nothing, you will find a boss who pays you nothing.
- If you ignore your feelings, you will get a job where people ignore your feelings. Maybe you'll join the army where people shout at you! It's not about THEM; it's about your relationship with YOU.
- If you hate your big backside, you will find a boyfriend who laughs at your big butt. When you accept your backside you will likely a) change boyfriends or b) discover that your old boyfriend has a new attitude.

  It was never about your boyfriend. It was always about your attitude toward you.
- If your boss demands better results, if your wife wants more from you, it is usually because in your heart, you want more from you.
- Even racial prejudice and religious prejudice isn't about THEM. When you accept you, people accept you.

If you love yourself, people will love you.

In a Nutshell

You create your world. You don't have to convince anybody else. You just have to feel different.

The Perfect Evening

Life is always reflecting back to us how we feel.

EXAMPLE: You have friends in town. You decide to treat them to a great evening at your favourite restaurant, Coco's.

You call the restaurant to book a table. The maître d' says, "Sorry, we're full."

"What do you mean, you're full?"

"We're booked out."

"But I'm a regular! Fit me in somewhere!"

'I'm sorry."

You slam down the phone. "Damn it! This should have been a great evening." You're angry.

You choose another restaurant. The food is greasy, the oysters stink, you argue with your wife all the way home and you wake up with food poisoning.

OR ...

The maître d' at Coco's says, "We're full."

You say, "Great. We've eaten there twenty times anyway. We should try something else." You call your ex-boss who knows all the best restaurants. He recommends a new place that is even closer.

The food is unforgettable. You chat with the couple at the next table and discover that they are your neighbours. You make some new friends, and next week you all go to Coco's.

Isn't this how life works?

If you believe that life is against you, it is. There is another way to live: believe that the Universe is plotting to make you happy.

In a Nutshell

The harmony you seek is not with other people; it is with yourself.

We Attract What We Fear

For my tenth birthday my Grandpa gave me a watch. In the 1960s watches weren't cheap! I was so proud and a little nervous. I thought, "I had better not break this!"

When I showered that night I placed my brand new Timex carefully on the sink beside my pyjamas. I washed and dried myself – and as I picked up my pyjamas, the sleeve knocked my beautiful birthday present face-down onto the tile floor. It shattered. I was shattered.

My first watch: given to me at 6.30, smashed by 8.15. I cried and cried. How could life be so cruel?

How often do we buy something new and damage it within hours? When is our fear strongest? When something is brand new.

Last month my tennis buddy, Aldo, bought a brand new Mazda SUV, and within forty-eight hours some vandal scratched the entire left side with a key. That same week my friend, Frank, bought a Honda. Within twenty-four hours a lady remodelled his back bumper in the mall car park.

How often have you found yourself in precisely the situation that you didn't want? You said to yourself, "If there is one thing I don't want to happen ... if there is one question I don't want to be asked ... if there is one mistake that I don't want to repeat ..." and guess what you got?

We attract what we fear.

Hell on the Highway

Have you had this experience? You drive to work every day for five years without incident. Then one morning you carelessly pull in front of a bus and almost cause an accident. You are in shock. Breathing hard, feeling vulnerable and stupid, you say to yourself, "This road is dangerous!" You keep driving.

Within five minutes a truck swerves into your lane. You avoid it, but only just. Now you are in a cold sweat. Ten minutes later a kid on a bike almost collects your front fender. You have had no near-accidents in five years – and then three near-misses in twenty minutes!

Everything you experience comes about because you are feeling confident, nervous, vulnerable, inadequate, excited, loved; you are creating your reality.

We don't have accidents; we construct them, thought by thought – "I'm a victim", "I hate this", "This is dangerous" – and then one day, "Whammo".

Does this sound cruel, blunt, scary? It is physics, and it is great news. Would you rather believe that, regardless of anything you think and feel, you have no protection from disease and no defence against accidents?

> *Some preachers tell you to fear God. That has to be a recipe for disaster!*

You are more than a physical body with a brain. You are a magnet, a transmitter. When you are joyful, happy and grateful, you somehow connect with other people and experiences that match your energy. It's the same when you are feeling vulnerable or scared.

See Yourself Protected

Many people like to imagine themselves as divinely protected. They make it a habit. When they are walking through a rough neighbourhood or driving on the highway, they will visualise themselves as surrounded by a protective white light.

When I first heard about this, I wondered, "How would that help against a mugger or a runaway truck?" Now I understand. The value in visualising the protective white light is that it changes how you feel. When you feel calm and protected, you are protected.

The Bible says, "Resist not evil." [23] It means *don't focus on bad stuff*. It means *don't spend your life thinking about illness and car crashes*. Rather, fill your mind with thoughts of health and happiness.

Some preachers tell you to fear God. That has to be a recipe for disaster!

In a Nutshell

If you think about what you want, you attract it.
If you think about what you don't want, you attract it.

How important Is Action?

11

You may ask, "What is more important? Thoughts and feelings? Or action?"

Look at it this way. When you build a house, you create a solid foundation that no one sees, and on that solid foundation you erect what everyone sees – the house.

The same principle works for whatever you want to do. If you want to find a wife, write a best-seller, start a company, have surgery or cycle safely through Europe, you need a solid foundation.

You create that SOLID FOUNDATION IN YOUR IMAGINATION with positive feelings of your goal happily achieved. On that invisible foundation you build what the world sees.

Many people forget the foundations. They are all *action and effort*. They race around trying to make something happen on no foundation, and the walls keep falling in.

Why an Invisible Foundation?

Without the feeling of your goal already achieved, you are broadcasting all kinds of feelings of doubt and uncertainty – feelings like, "This might be hard! What if I can't do it?" Then you attract experiences that match your feelings. It's a recipe for exhaustion. It's the reason that some talented people – golfers with perfect swings and singers with perfect pitch – settle for flipping hamburgers.

When you have the feeling of your goal ALREADY achieved, you become a magnet for the right people, books, websites and coincidences. Doors open. You don't have to lay every brick yourself. It is called synchronicity.

EXAMPLE: You plan a vacation. Your foundation is *you being excited and uplifted, getting the feeling of meeting fascinating people, tasting exotic food, returning healthy and refreshed.* You set it up in your mind. Your thoughts create the feeling. Your feelings – and then the action you take – create the experience.

Without the foundation, you are just a leaf in the wind. Anything might happen.

EXAMPLE: You need to make a difficult phone call. Your foundation *is the feeling of the goal achieved, the feeling that you made that call and you were confident and relaxed.* You create it in your mind FIRST. The creation is fun. The phone call becomes a breeze.

The imagining is a joy; the doing becomes a joy. That is how life is meant to work.

It All Sounds Too Easy

Let's say that you have been out of work for a year. You applied for sixty jobs and got sixty rejections. You are paralysed with disappointment.

A friend says, "Read this book, *How Life Works.*" You read it. You say, "This is nuts! Are you saying that if I just *feel good,* a job will drop in my lap?"

No. This is how it may happen.

Right now, you have given up. The idea of your getting a job seems IMPOSSIBLE. So you first need to change how you feel.

You begin to picture yourself as being happily employed. You imagine yourself excited to go to work each day. You imagine having a regular wage – and how your life will change. You wrap yourself in these happy feelings, fifty times a day.

You begin to affirm to yourself, *"I am so glad that I have a job."*

At first, all this seems a little ridiculous, but as you continue to imagine and affirm, the idea of your being employed starts to feel like a REMOTE POSSIBILITY.

Now that you are feeling more optimistic, it is easier to take action. You go online and study what to say at a job interview. You buy a book, *How to Get a Job.* You ask a friend to help you rewrite your CV.

You start looking at *Positions Vacant* online. You send out twenty applications and attend two interviews. You don't get hired, but you are more confident than before.

A friend of a friend gives you three days of part-time work. You are feeling better about yourself. The idea of your having a job seems POSSIBLE.

You attend another interview. The company calls you to say, "You are one of the final contenders."

Another guy gets the job, but you say to yourself, "At least I am being taken seriously."

A job now feels like a PROBABILITY; it's just a matter of when. You send out another twenty applications. Nineteen companies aren't interested. One company invites you for an interview. You nail it. The job is yours. (It's not over!)

You work hard for the next year. You feel more confident. Soon enough, you are ready for new challenges.

You apply for jobs at three different companies. You get hired at the third. (It's much easier to get a job this time.)

You work two years in the new company, and then one day, out of the blue, you get a phone call. A rival corporation offers you a position. You have been head-hunted! Now the jobs are chasing you!

This is how life gets better, step by step.

You say, "But what if there is a global financial crisis? Or what if I am sixty years old?"

Not all companies participate in global financial crises. Not all bosses want *young people*. When you have the unshakeable knowing that *"I am in demand"*, life will connect you with people who want your services, regardless of what you read in the papers. As Buddha might have said, "Your job is not in the world. Your job is in you."

> As Buddha might have said, "Your job is not in the world. Your job is in you."

Whether you are looking for work or a life partner, whether you want to lose 10 kilograms or learn to like yourself, you FIRST begin to change how you feel. Then you take action. You feel better. You take more action. This is how you get from IMPOSSIBLE to POSSIBLE to PROBABLE to ACHIEVED.

In a Nutshell

There are two parts to the equation: feel good + take action. The ancient Sufi proverb says; *"Trust in Allah, but first tie your camel to a post."*

MATTHEWS

What We Really Believe

How do you know what someone *really believes?* It's not in what they say. It's in what they DO.

We all know people who dream but take no action. They don't DO anything because *they expect to fail.* So they stay stuck. You can't fool the Universe.

Action demonstrates belief. For example:

● When you save money every week, you confirm your belief that a debt-free life is possible

- When you make a sales call, you confirm your belief that a sale is possible
- When you lift weights, you confirm your belief that fitness is possible
- When you give to the poor, you confirm your belief that more is coming.

Action is thought in motion.

Action accelerates results.

In a Nutshell

Fred may tell you, "I deserve a better life!" Fred may announce to the world, "I will be successful."

But unless Fred is taking action, he doesn't really believe it – and nothing will change.

Excellence

You say, "What about skill? Don't you have to be good at what you do?" Excellence is critical. The most successful people are very skilled.

And feeling good is part of the process.

When you feel optimistic and enthusiastic, when you continue to picture your goals achieved and when you continue to believe, these things happen:

- You are confident
- You attract the right colleagues, coaches, mentors and partners
- You attract opportunities
- You joyfully refine your skills.

The Law of Least Effort

The Indian Vedic texts from around 1500 BC explain the *Law of Cause and Effect (karma)*, the *Law of Detachment* and the *Law of Least Effort*.

The Law of Least Effort is perhaps least understood. As Vedic wisdom explains it, *love is the fabric that holds the Universe together.* This means:

- When you are motivated by LOVE and when you are serving others, you are in harmony with the Universe and your plans unfold with much less effort. Small miracles occur to help you on your way.

- When you are motivated by EGO, for example, if your aim is to be *the most powerful person in town* or if your business is *selling dodgy used cars to unsuspecting customers* or if your aim is *to control and impress people*, you will encounter endless resistance. "Success" will come at a price.

Self-help books may tell us, *"The sky is the limit. Go and do whatever you want!"* but you will notice a pattern: when our ambitions are largely selfish, life becomes a struggle.

In a Nutshell

When we are motivated by love, it takes LESS ACTION to produce MORE RESULTS.

The universal laws remind us that we are here to help each other.

Resistance

12

Groundhog Day

In the movie, *Groundhog Day*, Phil Connors is an angry, resentful TV weatherman. Each day when his alarm sounds at 6 am it is February 2nd. He is living the *same day!*

Phil tries everything to escape. He quits his job, he gets arrested, he attempts suicide six times – he drives off a cliff, leaps off a tall building, walks in front of a truck, gets shot, gets frozen and electrocutes himself in the bath – and when he wakes up tomorrow, it is yesterday!

Eventually, Phil learns to accept where he is. He starts to find beauty in the ordinary people in the little town of Punxsutawney.

It is a crazy comedy about a guy who is stuck in a time loop, re-living the worst day of his life. On another level, it has a deep message.

Groundhog Day is a perfect illustration of how resentment keeps us stuck, and love sets us free.

It's Not What Happens to You ...

It's not WHAT HAPPENS TO YOU that matters most. It's HOW YOU FEEL about what happens to you.

EXAMPLE: Let's say that you are at the airport, waiting to catch a flight, and the airline tells you, "Sorry! Mechanical trouble. You won't be leaving for three hours." You get very angry. You tell yourself: "This is terrible! I'll miss my connecting flight. This is a disaster!"

> *When you fight life, life always wins.*

While you remain stressed, things will get worse. People will trip over you, spill coffee in your lap and lose your baggage. When you fight life, life always wins!

Then finally you cool down. You tell yourself, "There's nothing I can do about it. I am probably where I am meant to be. I'll make the most of it."

Suddenly, everything changes! From nowhere an old friend appears, or you make a new friend, or you stumble on a fresh opportunity, and life begins to support you. Once we change our thoughts about "a bad situation", we can take advantage of it.

EXAMPLE: Imagine two women, Mary and Jane. Both get divorced.

Mary says, "I've failed. My life is over."

Jane says, "My life has just begun!"

Who will blossom?

In a Nutshell

Every "disaster" in your life is not so much a disaster, as a situation waiting for you to change your mind about it.

© ANDREW MATTHEWS

Crises

Life's great opportunities often arrive disguised as misfortune and disaster.

When have you made the most important decisions in your life? Isn't it when you were on your knees, following disasters or knockbacks, and you said, "I never want to be this broke anymore," or "I never want to be in this kind of relationship anymore."?

- When do we usually fix our diet or start exercising?
  When our body is falling apart.
- When do couples tell each other how much they love each other?
  When the relationship is falling apart.
- When do we make critical financial decisions?
  When we can't pay our bills.
- When do we back up our computers?
  After we have lost everything!

We know it all until:

- we have a heart attack
- we go broke
- the love of our life leaves.

> *The good thing about a crisis is that we become teachable.*

The good thing about a crisis is that we become desperate – and teachable.

Funny, isn't it? We spend our lives trying to accumulate stuff, but we learn most when we lose it.

In a Nutshell

Success we celebrate. Failure we contemplate.
We learn most from pain and disappointment.

Pain

We suffer pain when we believe something that is not true. For example, we suffer pain when we believe:

- "I AM MY JOB," for example, "I am a teacher," or "I am a doctor." If you think you are your job, then, when you don't have one, you feel like you have disappeared. When you know *you are not your job*, you aren't shattered, just inconvenienced.
- "I AM MY BANK BALANCE." No! Your self-worth is not equal to your net worth.
- "I AM MY BODY." You have one, but you are not it.
- "I AM MY REPUTATION." No. Your reputation is what *other people think*. You are not what other people think.
- "I AM HELPLESS AND OUT OF CONTROL." Absolutely and entirely wrong!
- "I AM WORTHLESS." Wrong again. See the rest of this book.

In a Nutshell

Pain is often a message
to change our thinking.

Death

When we think that life should be a certain way – and it isn't – it hurts. One reason why people think *life is unfair* is because they think *death is unfair*. People who believe *life is terrible* often believe *death is terrible*.

The idea that death is terrible stems from beliefs like:

- everyone should live at least 75 years, and any less is a tragedy
- death is the end of it.

But is your death the end of you?

I tend to take notice of experts. When people dedicate their lives to making movies or managing corporations or performing heart surgery, I figure they know something I don't.

Here's what I notice about those joyous people who have dedicated themselves to a spiritual life: they all say roughly the same thing.

- You are an eternal spirit in a body
- Life is wonderful
- You came here to experience joy and realise your true power
- There are no accidents; we leave this planet when we are ready
- Don't be so serious!

If you try to figure this all out intellectually, it probably doesn't make sense. If you just live it, it works beautifully.

How Much Time Do You Need?

It may seem reasonable that we should all get at least 75 years on Earth, but the fact is, we don't. Some lives are short. Humanity is about variety. We each think differently, live differently. Not all guys look like Brad Pitt.

As heartbreaking as it is to lose loved ones unexpectedly, it seems that some people do their thing quickly and move on. Some beautiful, angelic, four-year-olds come for just a brief visit.

Some people evolve quickly. Some hang on for 95 years.

In a Nutshell

We are each a divine, loving, powerful spirit in a body. When we forget this, life hurts. It is life's way of getting us back on track.

Let Go!

13

My friend, Caroline, has spent her life managing exotic hotels around the world – island getaways on the Great Barrier Reef, elephant sanctuary resorts in northern Thailand, breathtaking properties on Sydney Harbour and even a hotel-that-used-to-be-a-palace in the Himalayas.

Here's what fascinates me about Caroline. She has spent her life managing luxurious hotels and yet she has:

- no training in hospitality or hotel management
- never had a CV
- never been out of work.

Caroline recently retired after her fourteenth management position in thirty years, none of which she applied for. It's not luck.

Why is Caroline such a magnet for opportunity? She has absolutely no fear of being unemployed. She is totally detached. Her experience in the workplace is different from most people's because *her thinking* is different from most people's.

She says, "It's crazy. I'm not a great manager, but these jobs just happen. I live in blind trust. I know that the right job will always come at the right time."

Chasing Girlfriends, Chasing Dogs

The Buddhists teach detachment. You know about it. When we chase girlfriends, boyfriends, even dogs, they run away. Why? Because we are chasing them! When we try to trap people in relationships, they can't wait to escape! When we LET GO, they often come back!

> *When you stop trying to sell it, everyone wants to buy it!*

Did you ever spend weeks searching for an apartment but found nothing you liked? After endless frustration you quit looking – and that's when you found your new home. As soon as you signed the lease, you discovered three more perfect apartments without even looking!

Did you ever want to sell something – a stroller, a laptop, a parachute? Nobody wanted it, and so you gave it away. When you stopped trying to sell it, everyone wanted to buy it.

We talked about lack thoughts in Chapter 8. Desperation and LACK THOUGHTS are part of the same mindset. If we can't find an apartment, or a job or a plane ticket – and we become desperate – we continue creating the same lack experience.

Once we get the job, the apartment or the boyfriend, our thinking shifts from "I need this" to "I have what I need". "I have what I need" is a totally different vibration. "I have what I need" is your most powerful state. "I have what I need" is the starting point for a much easier life.

Fred says, "But you don't get it! I *don't have* what I need! When I *have* what I need, then I'll be grateful; then I'll be happy." Perfectly understandable, Fred, but the results of this approach are always disappointing.

In a Nutshell
The trick to the game of life is to feel happy, grateful and detached.

Detachment

Detachment is not disinterest. It is possible to be detached and still be very determined. People who are detached *and* determined know that *effort and excellence are ultimately rewarded.* They say: *"If I don't win this time, I'll win the next time, or the time after that."*

Let's say you apply for a position at Loony Larry's Laptops. You are excited about the job and you prepare carefully. You write out your interview speech and you practise it in front of the bathroom mirror. You even get a haircut. You arrive early for the interview and you give it your best shot.

What next? You get on with your life. You enrol in extra study. You plan your next job application. If you get hired by Loony Larry, you're happy. If not, you are still moving forward.

Disinterested people say: *"Who cares, and why bother?"*

Desperate people say: *"If I don't get this I'll die!"*

When you are determined and detached, you say: *"One way or another, I will get a good job – and I don't care how long it takes."*

ANDREW MATTHEWS

Nature doesn't understand desperation! Nature seeks balance, and you can't be desperate *and* balanced.

Life doesn't have to be an endless struggle. Let things flow. This is not indifference; it's not forcing things.

In a Nutshell

There's such a thing as trying too hard!

> *Life doesn't have to be an endless struggle.*

Giving

Churches tell us we should give, but they don't explain why giving is so magical. The secret to life is how we FEEL. Few things make us feel lighter and happier than giving someone a present, a compliment or a helping hand. When we give happily, we feel wonderful.

When we feel wonderful, we become a magnet for good things. So WHEN WE GIVE, WE CREATE A FLOW. It is that simple. No one ever explained this to me!

Here's a principle which seems to make no sense: *whatever it is that you most want, share it.* Give freely, wanting nothing in return. If you want money, share some of yours. If you want love, share yours. It's how you create a flow.

Take Mary who is desperate to be loved. Mary is angry with her husband, Fred. She says, "I do so much for Fred but he doesn't love me back!" Mary does do a lot for Fred – but she isn't loving him. She is counting everything she does. And she is keeping score: Mary, 10; Fred, 2.

When you are simply loving people with no strings attached, love comes back. It has to. It always will.

Give Happily

It matters HOW we give. If we give begrudgingly, we feel bad. When we feel bad, we don't receive abundance. That is why it is powerful to give anonymously.

Here is a fun game: send a friend a birthday card with fifty dollars in it – but don't sign the card. The game is to never let them know you sent it.

Your friend will be delighted and intrigued that money just came from nowhere. It's also a joy for you.

And here's the big benefit: you get to practise giving without needing thanks. You get to practise not caring whether people express appreciation or not. And when you don't NEED gratitude and appreciation? You get more of it.

In a Nutshell

It's not *what* you give; it's *how* you give.

Finding Your Life's Purpose

The Sanskrit word for *your purpose in life* is "dharma". According to the Law of Dharma, we each have unique talents that we are here to discover. When we express those talents, we find joy.

According to the law, we are most likely to discover those talents when we ask, "What can I give?" rather than, "What can I get back?"

When Everything Is Going Wrong

14

Rocky

Rocky is an angry young street fighter. He hangs around clubs and bars. Almost every week he gets into a street brawl, and he has the scars and the broken teeth to prove it.

Then Rocky has a brainwave: "I'll learn karate. Then I can beat up three people at once."

So Rocky enrolls in a gym. Rocky loves it, but the master tells him, "You are too angry! You can't fight when you're angry."

Rocky says, "That's how I am – ANGRY!"

But Rocky notices that he keeps getting thrashed at the gym by old guys who are half his size. Eventually, he learns some relaxation exercises. It helps. He gets quicker, his anticipation improves, but he doesn't know why. He doesn't realise that he is starting to harness his *subconscious mind*.

Rocky has seen those guys on YouTube who break bricks with their hands and smash concrete with their heads. Rocky thinks, "I want to smash some concrete!" He asks the master, "How do you do that?" The master says, "You do it with chi."

"What's chi?"

"Chi," says the master, "is the energy of the Universe. You have to become a channel for the power of the Universe. You need to learn to meditate." Rocky laughs. "Chi? That's crap."

Rocky goes home and puts a brick on his coffee table. He tries to smash it with his forehead and spends the weekend in hospital.

Rocky is puzzled. How come skinny little sixty-year-old guys can shatter lumps of concrete? And how could Bruce Lee knock a guy across the room with his *one-inch punch!*

Rocky really wants to smash things. So he learns to meditate. Rocky learns to focus his energy. He discovers that *thinking* doesn't help; rather, you express your intention and then you have to get your mind out of the way. And so he learns to break stuff – and it's weird; as he discovers his power, he becomes more humble.

Rocky notices something else: as he becomes more relaxed, he finds more peace of mind. For the first time in his life he begins to like himself. Rocky discovers that people like him, and he likes people. He makes some friends. One day it dawns on Rocky, "I don't get into street fights anymore."

Rocky helps other angry young kids. He understands those kids. In fact, he loves them. Often he'll tell them, "I used to be like you."

And one day Rocky hears himself explaining to a young teen, "You don't have to impress anybody. You aren't here to teach anyone a lesson. You are here to learn about yourself. Relax. Stay in the moment and you become a channel for the energy of the Universe."

Rocky explains, "As you learn how to fight, so you learn about yourself. When you have mastered yourself, there is no one left to fight."

And the kid says, "That's crap."

In a Nutshell

Sometimes you can get into something – a job, a marriage or the science of how to beat up other people – for all the *wrong reasons,* and emerge with *all the right answers.*

"This is a disaster!"

When I first learned about the Law of Attraction I was single. I began to imagine my perfect wife: beautiful, smart, funny, feminine and not too tall. A couple of years went by. I kept visualising her, but she still hadn't shown up. I began to wonder, "How long does this take? Where is she?"

At that time I was running weekend seminars. I had rent, wages, advertising costs, electrical bills, printing and postage costs. I needed eighteen people in a seminar to pay my bills. My courses averaged about thirty people, and so I was doing okay. Then one November, I just couldn't get the numbers – and even the people who *had* booked were all dropping out.

Soon I was down to twelve. No matter what I did, I just couldn't fill the room. I thought, "This is a disaster!" Eventually, I had to tell myself, "You have done all that you can. Whatever happens, happens." I stopped struggling. In my mind I stopped complaining. I let go.

> *Life-changing relationships and opportunities appear when we least expect them.*

And into that seminar of twelve people walked the woman of my dreams. That was 1986. We married in 1991.

Julie is my inspiration. She is the smartest, most elegant, most generous, most courageous, most extraordinary woman I ever met – all 150cm of her.

This is my experience: life-changing relationships and opportunities appear when we least expect them. It is life's way of saying, "Never underestimate the present moment."

In a Nutshell

When we think everything is going wrong, it usually isn't. We just can't see the whole picture.

Your Radar Screen

Our conscious mind is like a tiny radar screen that sees just a fraction of what is going on around us.

We are always surrounded by people, events and possibilities approaching us that we can't see on the radar. Because we can't see them with our physical senses, we think they aren't there.

But they are there. And every time you have a positive feeling about love or money or a happy life, what you feel good about moves closer. But it is only at the very END of the creation process that what you are feeling appears on your screen.

People who struggle and suffer and complain believe that the radar screen is all there is. But our radar screen is picking up just the tiniest corner of our Universe.

Julie was always out there and always getting closer. It just took me two years to get her onto my radar.

In a Nutshell

All those things that you have been feeling excited about are still moving toward you. You just need to keep the feeling until you land them on your screen.

Go with the Flow

Life is like riding a stream. Some people spend their life swimming against the current. Some people thrash about in a permanent panic. Some people never jump in.

It is easier to go with the flow. The more flexible you are, the better you feel and the better life works.

Money will sometimes be tight and sometimes be plentiful. People will sometimes promise more than they deliver. You will have days when it seems everything is going wrong.

On those tough days, as on every day, affirm to yourself, "Everything will work out fine!"

In a Nutshell

You cannot control everything.

You don't have to control everything.

You don't have to know HOW things will work out.

Acceptance

15

Where Energy Comes from

Imagine this: you didn't sleep last night. You were up at 4 am and you had a long day at the office. You fought the boss and you fought the traffic. It's now 6 pm and you are home, collapsed on the sofa, too tired to shower and too tired to eat.

Your phone rings, and it's a very official-sounding lady. She verifies your name and address and says, "We have been trying to contact you all day. *Congratulations! You are the winner of the state lottery – the sum of twenty million dollars."*

You leap three feet in the air. "Twenty million! We're RICH!"

You race up and down the stairs to find the family. You call your mother, your brother, all your friends and neighbours. "Get over here! Let's party!"

QUESTION: Where did you get all the energy from? It had to come from somewhere!

You say, "It's the money!" But it's not the money. You haven't even got it yet. And it could be a hoax.

Here's where the energy came from: energy flows into your being every time you say, "THIS IS A GREAT MOMENT!" It is how life works. It is the cosmic difference between "Oh, YES!" and "Oh, no!"

It's why three-year-olds are unstoppable. To three-year-olds, everything is fresh and exciting. They are energy channels. If you could get a three-year-old to worry about mortgages and medical bills, he would be as tired as his grandparents.

> *Energy flows into your being every time you say, "This is a GREAT MOMENT!"*

Blockages

The Chinese understand energy. Chinese medicine explains why, when you get angry with your boyfriend, you get a raging headache. You tense up in your neck and shoulders, you choke off the energy flow in your "meridians" and you get a pain in your head.

Whenever we resist a situation, whenever we say, "This is not okay," we block energy flow.

Massage or acupuncture removes the blockage. (So does forgiving your boyfriend.) You relax, the energy flows and there is no more headache.

We are all channels – we channel energy and inspiration. The word, "enthusiasm", comes from the Latin, "enthusiasmus", meaning *divine inspiration, possessed by a god*. When we are enthusiastic, we have life force flowing through us and we are connected to everything. But every time we say, "This is a bad moment!", every time we find fault, every time we judge people and events, we clog our channel.

When electricity can't travel down a wire or past a piece of plastic tape, we say there is "resistance". When there is enough resistance, electrical energy stops flowing altogether.

It's the same with you. When energy can't flow into you, it's due to a blockage, or resistance. How do we recognise resistance? It sounds something like this:

- "I hate this traffic."
- "I hate my job."
- "I'm always broke."
- "I might get sick!"
- "I should have married her sister!"

Saving Energy

You can't save up your energy like money in a bank. The less you love, the less love flows through you. The less energy you spend, the less energy flows through you.

Misery and apathy shut off your energy. That is why depressed people are mostly exhausted. Passion for life and people restores the flow.

How to Stay Stuck

Here's how to stay stuck in any job, situation or relationship: look for things that are wrong.

The more reasons you can find to be disappointed or resentful, the more resistance you create, and the more slowly your life will move. You are not being punished; you are simply choking off your life force.

You say, "Do I need to be more tolerant?" No! Tolerance is resistance: it's simply more polite. *"I don't like this, but I'm suffering in silence!"*

We need to move from tolerance to …

Acceptance

> **Today I will judge nothing that occurs.** [24]
> ***A Course in Miracles***

Perhaps you are broke right now. Perhaps you have lost your job or lost a loved one. Maybe you are sick. You say, "I just don't know what to do."

Here is the first thing to do: accept where you are. To turn things around, you first make peace with your situation. Forget about blame, forget about guilt, forget the "what ifs". Progress depends on acceptance.

Acceptance doesn't mean, "I want to stay here." Acceptance means, "This is where I am – and now I move on to what I want."

Instead of, "My marriage is a mess and I'm angry and resentful," it is more like, "My marriage is a mess. What a perfect learning experience! Now my life can begin to get better."

Acceptance isn't *giving up*. Acceptance is recognition that "This is a part of my journey". Very often it means, "Right now *I have no idea* why this had to be a part of my journey, but I embrace it anyway." "I needed to be here" doesn't mean "I need to stay here."

In a Nutshell
Logic will tell you, "If I accept this rotten moment I will be stuck with it forever!" In fact, the reverse is true. Acceptance allows you to move on.

How Do I Practice Acceptance?
Do you want to prove to yourself that positive thinking works?

Try this: every morning when you wake up, say "This is perfect. Where I am is perfect. All my mistakes are perfect. My life until now is the perfect preparation to graduate to something better."

Does the word, "perfect", seem too extreme? Then try using the word, "okay". Whenever things seem to go wrong – you miss a flight, you lose your house keys, you miss out on a promotion – tell yourself, "I don't know why, but this is okay!" And then look for reasons to be happy now.

What will happen? Your energy will change and your life will change.

What happens when you accept what IS? Frustration dissolves into fascination. You still have challenges, but they resolve themselves almost effortlessly. You argue less, you quit trying to make other people wrong, you quit complaining. You look for good things, and as you look for good things, life heaps more good things upon you. Friends, lovers and opportunities appear almost magically. You get the feeling that the Universe is plotting to make you happy.

> *"I needed to be here" doesn't mean "I need to stay here."*

To have a beautiful life, you don't have to know everything about everything and you don't even have to be very smart! It is more about accepting where you are, seeing the best in people and believing life will turn out well.

In a Nutshell
Acceptance is power.

Forgiveness

16

Where do we get the idea that if WE don't forgive people, THEY suffer? It's nuts!

Let's say:

a) you are my boss and you give me the sack; or

b) you are my girl and you run off with my best friend.

So I say, "I'll never forgive you for that!" Who suffers? Not you! I'm pacing the floor. I've got the headaches and the indigestion. I'm losing sleep. You are probably out *partying!*

If I don't forgive you, it ruins MY life!

Is forgiveness easy? Usually not. It is hard to forgive people because when we try to forgive, we focus on what "they did". So we keep getting more and more angry!

So here's a thought that may be helpful: don't even TRY to forgive people. Just look for their good qualities, look for things to appreciate in them. If you can find one quality and concentrate on that, sooner or later you will find something else to appreciate, and something else. And as you see more and more good things, your relationship will heal.

As your relationship heals, the past will take care of itself.

To forgive people, you don't have to agree with what they did. You just have to want your life to work.

> *To forgive people you don't have to agree with what they did.*

In a Nutshell

You don't forgive people for their benefit.

You do it for your benefit.

And there's more to it …

It Takes Two

If I believe that:

- life is unfair
- everybody is a cheat
- all bosses are bullies

I will attract experiences that prove my belief system. People will appear in my life to empty my bank account, break my nose or leave me stranded at the altar. My low-quality thoughts will deliver low-quality experiences.

Do I *want* the unhappy experiences? No.

Do I choose those *exact experiences*? No.

But by the quality of my feelings I determine the QUALITY of my experiences.

So if, for example, Jim comes along and smacks me in the mouth, Jim is simply a perfect match for how I feel about myself at the moment. If it wasn't Jim, then it would have been a neighbour or a perfect stranger who belted me.

IT IS NOT ABOUT JIM. I created the "window" for a smack in the mouth. One person who is feeling bad about himself attracts another person who feels like thumping someone. Perfect!

So does it make sense to blame Jim if I created the conditions for Jim to thump me? And the answer is, "No."

At this point you might say, "Wait! This is ridiculous! What kind of idiot would say, '*Never* blame other people?'."

And the answer is: EVERY SPIRITUAL MASTER WHO EVER LIVED because they understand how life works.

MATTHEWS

"Stop beating yourself up."

- People appear to be ruining your life as long as you believe they are ruining your life
- You are creating your life experience.

Your beliefs keep you stuck right where you are.

In a Nutshell

You don't forgive people because it's holy or spiritual. You forgive people because it is PRACTICAL. Resenting people keeps you STUCK. Forgiveness sets you free. And there's more ...

Forgive Yourself!

It is not *other people* that we blame the most – it is ourselves.

Most of us had parents who didn't feel good about themselves. So they found fault with us. So we grew up believing:

- "I am stupid"
- "I'm too fat, skinny, ugly, short ..."

"I need to prove myself."

We also have that Voice in our head – the *Inner Critic*. The Inner Critic is an invisible bully, forever stalking us, tearing us down.

- "You're not smart enough, you're not loveable, you're not beautiful."
- "You need to make more money, get more stuff, win more trophies, be more impressive."
- 'You should be more like your brother, sister, father, neighbour."

Silencing the Inner Critic

You ask, "So how do I silence my Inner Critic?"

For the last fifty years, psychologists and therapists have told us, "Raise your self-esteem! When you feel better about yourself, the Critic will leave you alone."

But here's the problem: we try to raise our self-esteem by comparing ourselves with other people. We tell ourselves:

- "I'm okay because I'm thinner than her."
- "I'm okay because I got a promotion, won a trophy, drive an Audi."
- "I'm okay because I'm above average."

But we all can't be above average! And we can't be above average at everything.

Self-esteem works when everything is going well. But how do you maintain a good self-image when you just got sacked or divorced – or when you are battling addiction? It's like trying to run a marathon with a broken leg.

Self-compassion

Many experts now recommend another way. It's called self-compassion – where we quit thrashing ourselves and quit comparing ourselves with other people.

With self-compassion, we stop asking questions like, *"How am I different? How am I better?"* We begin asking the question, *"How am I the same as everyone else?"*

We give ourselves permission to be imperfect. We take time to notice when we are hurting. Interestingly, the less we criticise ourselves, the more effective we become. The less we compete with people, the more we connect with people.

How does self-compassion help? Here's the crunch:

- If I CRITICISE myself I feel bad. When I feel bad, life beats up on me: I get jilted, cheated, exploited and exhausted.
- If I ACCEPT myself, I feel good. When I feel good, I get loved and appreciated. I get opportunities. Things work out.

"I need to make more money, win more trophies, prove I'm right..."

There are many helpful books and websites about practising self-compassion, including www.compassionfocusedtherapy.com.au and www.self-compassion.org.

The Secret to Feeling Loved

Socialogist Brené Brown, PhD[25], spent ten years studying people who feel loved and people who feel unloved. So what is the difference? Are loved people more beautiful, more intelligent or more trendy? Do unloved people make more blunders? No.

Here's what Brown discovered: PEOPLE WHO FEEL LOVED BELIEVE THEY DESERVE TO BE LOVED. It is that simple.

If you have made stupid mistakes, guilt won't fix them. If you are imperfect, join the club. If you want to feel loved, forgive yourself for not being perfect.

There is Only One Relationship

Your relationships are not about your boss, your girlfriend, your family and friends. Your happiness is not dependent on THEM. There is only one relationship that matters, and that is how you feel about you. The rest are mirrors.

No one ever had a hit record, won a tournament, or kept a job or a friendship who didn't believe they deserved it. No one was ever loved for a lifetime who didn't believe they were worthy of love.

In a Nutshell

The problem is not that God judges you; the problem is that you judge you.

Your Miraculous Body

17

If you give any group of patients a simple sugar pill to cure asthma, depression or an allergy, about 33% will report improvement or a cure. Medicine calls this the *placebo effect*.

You say, "Okay, placebos might work for things that are *in the mind* – like depression – but what about REAL problems? What about something physical like osteoarthritis?"

Fake Surgery

Orthopedic surgeon, Dr Bruce Moseley, was the lead author of a Baylor School of Medicine study[26] that set out to determine which of two common surgical procedures gave greater relief to patients suffering from severe knee pain.

There were 180 patients in the study, divided into three groups of 60:

- Group A got surgery: Moseley shaved the damaged cartilage of the knee
- Group B got surgery: Moseley flushed out the damaged knee joint, and removed any material that might be causing the pain
- Group Placebo got fake surgery. Moseley made three incisions in the skin, *pretended* to operate and then sewed up the incisions after forty minutes.

Group Placebo were allowed to believe they had had real surgery for two years before they were finally told, "We tricked you. You had no surgery!"

And the results?

Groups A and B that had the real surgery improved as expected. For Group Placebo that had NO surgery, their improvement was EQUAL to those who *had* surgery. One member of the placebo group, Tim Perez, had been restricted to walking with a cane. Following the fake surgery, he was able to play basketball with his grandchildren.

Dr Moseley observes, *"The bigger the treatment the patient thinks they're going to have, the bigger the placebo effect, and in general small pills don't have as big of a placebo effect as bigger pills, and pills don't have as big of an effect as shots, and shots don't have as big of an effect as procedures ..."* [27] The power of belief!

This shouldn't surprise us. The first placebo trial was conducted in 1801 and medical research has continued to demonstrate the same phenomena ever since.

How can this be? Here's what we do know for sure: whether your ulcer heals, whether you cure your depression or whether the arthritic pain in your knee disappears depends much on what you believe. This raises some questions.

If placebos work for a third of patients, why don't they work for all patients?

Perhaps it is because real drugs don't work for all patients, either. Belief is part of the equation and some patients don't believe they can be cured. And strange as it may sound, some patients don't want to be cured.

Why do placebos work?

A sugar tablet or an imaginary operation gives you expectation and hope, and when you have belief your energy changes. When you feel better, you heal better.

When people discover that a placebo helped their bodies heal, they are usually embarrassed, as if to say, "A sugar pill made me better! It was all in my mind. Am I crazy?"

What we should say is, "A sugar pill made me better. I am miraculous!"

How can the mind influence the cells of the body to effect a cure when we don't even know what our body needs to do to fix the problem?

That's just it. You never have had a clue about how your body works.

When you cut your finger, do you have to think about making a scab, creating scar tissue, mending and growing capillaries? When you eat a pizza, do you have to concentrate on digesting that last anchovy? What do you know about replacing your entire stomach lining (which happens every two days) or producing bile or growing fingernails?

Right now the cells in your body are digesting, breathing, expelling waste, making proteins, replicating your DNA, watching out for toxins and predators, sending messages. There are 100,000 chemical reactions happening in EACH cell of your body every second.

Each cell is like an entire universe. In just one cell in your nostril, your liver or your rectum, there are 6 trillion things happening every second.

You have 50 trillion cells in your body; so that's 300,000,000, 000,000,000,000,000,000 things happening in your body every second. And how much do you know about it?

It is your subconscious mind that takes care of it. You are a PASSENGER.

But It's My Genes!

You say, "Okay, but there must be a limit to what the mind can do. Isn't our health determined by our genes?"

In the 1960s, long before most of us had even heard of genetics, Dr Bruce Lipton was already cloning stem cells and studying DNA. In his best-selling book, *The Biology of Belief,*[28] Lipton draws on almost fifty years of research to explain that we have gone overboard in assuming that our life is determined by our genes.

> *Your genes are not like some time bomb waiting to explode.*

Says Dr Lipton, your genes are only a blueprint for what MIGHT happen. A blueprint is a plan, a possibility. For example, if you have a blueprint to build a bookshelf, and you leave the blueprint in your briefcase, the bookshelf never gets built. The blueprint can't build the bookshelf. The necessary *environment* to build a bookshelf includes you and a screwdriver.

It is the same with your genes. Your genes are not like some time bomb waiting to explode. How your genes behave depends on the *environment*. Something has to switch your DNA on or off. What switches DNA on or off is the environment that you create with your lifestyle and your thoughts – at the quantum level at which matter appears and disappears.

Dr Lipton refers to the work of eminent scientist and physician, Dean Ormish. Says Lipton, *"Ormish revealed that by just changing diet and lifestyle for 90 days, prostate cancer patients switched the activity of over 500 genes."* [29]

Lipton continues, "Some people come here with defective genes and with their mind they can rewrite those genes and make them normal."

He explains, *"We do not have to go through the fate of our genes because we are masters of our genes. We are not victims unless our belief system says we are."*

That's why Dr Lipton named his book, *The Biology of Belief.*

Emotion

Traditionally, scientists don't acknowledge fuzzy things like emotions, but this is changing.

Renowned pharmacologist, Candace Pert PhD, has spent decades studying why we feel the way we feel.

Pert has published over 250 scientific papers. So what does a hard-nosed laboratory scientist have to say about how emotions interact with the "real" world? And how important are our feelings? Says Pert:

> **We can no longer think of the emotions as having less validity than material, physical substance but instead we must see them as cellular signals that are involved in the process of translating information into physical reality, literally transforming mind into matter.**[30]

Just as Einstein and quantum physics demonstrated that *all matter is energy*, Pert suggests that *all energy is information.* This is a useful way to picture your body and the rest of the Universe.

In a Nutshell

Western medicine is starting to embrace what Eastern medicine has known for 6,000 years.

- Negative thoughts are toxic
- Wellness and disease begin in the mind.

Your Heart

18

How often we talk about our hearts! We say someone has *a big heart, a light heart, a heavy heart, a hard heart, a soft heart, a black heart, a change of heart, a broken heart* or *no heart*. And no one ever says, "I love you with all my brain!"

Something else: when we point to ourselves, we never point our finger at our head. We point to our heart.

If feelings create our life experience, some logical questions arise.

- Does the heart emit a strong energy?
- Do traditional cultures recognise heart or feeling energy?
- Is the heart more than just a pump?

Can we measure energy from the heart?

This is a question posed by a group of scientists at the Institute of HeartMath: www.heartmath.com.

HeartMath[31] found that *"the heart produces by far the body's most powerful rhythmic electromagnetic field"*. This energy field is about three metres across and encircles your chest like a huge doughnut.

This electromagnetic *heart field* is 5,000 TIMES STRONGER than the field surrounding your brain. This is significant! Suddenly, the idea that *how you feel* shapes your destiny sounds a lot more reasonable.

A Mystery

Your heart not only knows things; it remembers them.

In the last 50 years we have learnt much about the brain but less about the heart. We don't know what starts the heart beating in the womb and we don't know why a heart can keep beating after it is disconnected from the brain.[32]

If you place *a group* of heart cells in a dish in a laboratory – with each of them separated – they will beat to a single rhythm. How do they do it? How do they know?

More Mysteries

Psychoneuroimmunologist, Paul Pearsall PhD, spent thirty years studying people who have had heart transplants. He amassed 140 reports and audio-tapes from patients who received other people's hearts.

In his best-seller, *The Heart's Code,*[33] he tells stories of patients who developed the behaviours and passions of their hearts' donors BEFORE THEY KNEW anything about the donors. For example:

- A thirty-five-year-old female recipient received the heart of a topless dancer. She reported that before the transplant, sex was not a big part of her life. After the operation she explained, "I want sex every night ... Now I tire my husband out ... I used to hate X-rated videos, now I love them ... I think I got *her* sexual drive."

- A fifty-two-year-old male who received the heart of a seventeen-year-old boy said, "I loved quiet classical music before my new heart. Now I put on earphones, crank up the stereo and play loud rock-and-roll music."

In her autobiography, *A Change of Heart,* Claire Sylvia[34] tells of her own transformation. Before receiving a heart and lung transplant, she was conservative and health-conscious. After her transplant she developed a passion for beer, chicken nuggets and motorbikes. When she spoke with the donor's family she discovered that she had been given the heart of a beer-drinking, chicken nugget-loving motorcyclist.

Dr Pearsall recounts the story of an eight-year-old girl who received the heart of a murdered ten-year-old girl. The eight-year-old began to have nightmares – and reported that she knew the identity of the killer of her heart's donor.

Police used descriptions and evidence provided by the eight-year-old to arrest the murderer, who was ultimately convicted. Reports Pearsall, "the time, the weapon, the place, the clothes he wore, what the little girl he killed had said to him ... everything the heart transplant recipient reported was completely accurate."[35]

How can this be?

An emerging view is that ALL cells – not just brain cells – have memory. DNA code is contained in every cell of your body. So, too, it seems, is memory.

The Western concept is that the brain is king and the heart is a pump. But the heart has a nervous system of its own. The heart is a conscious organ. Your heart not only knows things; it remembers them.

What Traditional Cultures Know

Traditional cultures know about *life force* or *heart energy.* There are over 100 words for it. The Polynesians call it *mana*, the Indians and Tibetans call it *prana*, the Iroquois call it *orendam*, the Ituri pygmies call it *megbe*, Chinese and Japanese medicine calls it *chi*.

Western medicine calls it baloney.

In the West we tend to worship the brain and ignore the heart. Western medicine has no words – and no place – for "life force", "prana" or "chi". And it is in the West that heart disease is out of control. Is nature trying to tell us something?

In a Nutshell

Your feelings are not just incidental by-products of your thoughts. Your feelings are your life force. They are your lifeline to the Universe.

Should this surprise us? The first organ to form in your mother's womb was your heart.

"I know my husband can be loving and kind.
He is that way with the dog."

We Are All Connected

19

Is it selfish to seek happiness?

Psychological tests prove that when you are happy, you are more likely to lend people money or carry their groceries. Similar tests prove that when you are miserable you are more likely to steal their wallet or kick a dog.

So *your happiness* benefits everyone around you and all the dogs in the neighbourhood.

It doesn't stop there …

Helping People at a Distance

During the Israeli-Lebanese War in 1983, Dr Charles N Alexander and Dr David Orme-Johnson[36] conducted a stunning study in Jerusalem.

They wanted to find out, "What happens when a group of people feel peaceful? And what happens if a group of people feel happy and peaceful in the middle of a war zone?"

For two months between August 1 and September 30, a group of meditators, ranging in number between 65 and 241, meditated twice daily in a hotel in East Jerusalem. Their mission was simply to come together and feel peace. And what happened?

During these two months, war deaths, terrorist attacks, fires, hospital emergencies and automobile accidents decreased markedly – in Lebanon, Jerusalem and Israel as a whole. There was a precise relationship.

Dr Alexander and Dr Orme-Johnson made a sophisticated analysis, accounting for variables such as weather, days of the week and holidays. The data showed that when the experiment began, violence decreased immediately. When more mediators participated, violence decreased further. When the experiment stopped, the violence returned to former levels.

Their research paper, *The International Peace Project in the Middle East,* is online.[37]

Similar studies to this have been conducted in Puerto Rico, in the Philippines, in Delhi, India and in twenty-four cities across the United States. It only takes a small group to make a difference – as few as a hundred people in a city of a million.

What Else?

You may ask, "If we are invisibly connected, shouldn't there be scientific evidence?" There is. Here are some examples.

- In 1988 Dr Randolph Byrd[38] conducted a study at the San Francisco General Hospital coronary care unit, demonstrating that heart patients who were prayed for by random groups scattered around the world recovered significantly better than patients who were not prayed for.

- Biofeedback expert, Dr Elmer Green,[39] has compared the electrostatic energy released from the bodies of ordinary people (10-15 millivolts) with the electrostatic energy released by meditators when they are meditating and healers when they are healing. He found healers produced voltages of up to 190 volts – or 100,000 times the normal amount.

- In 1966, Cleve Backster[40] connected a polygraph (lie detector) to a pot plant. He was curious to see whether his dracaena plant would react to being watered. When the polygraph recorded a small response, he wondered, "What would happen if I burned a leaf?" That is when the recording pen swung wildly and nearly jumped off the page. Backster hadn't even burned the plant yet! He had simply *thought about it*. Backster had stumbled onto something. He spent the next thirty years in research demonstrating that plants, mould cultures, eggs and even yoghurt have an awareness of their surroundings that he called "primary perception".

- Nobel Prize winner, Niels Bohr, discovered that, once sub-atomic particles have been in contact with each other, they remain forever influenced by each other. To explain, let's imagine two particles; we'll call them Bob and Alice. They spend one crazy night together in Rio, and then Bob moves to Miami. Here's what's amazing: whenever Bob changes the speed at which he is spinning, Alice will change, too. Even if Bob moves to the other side of the Universe, when Bob changes his speed of rotation, Alice will change, too, AT THE EXACT SAME INSTANT.

This phenomenon, where particles remain *linked forever,* is known in quantum physics as "entanglement". My quantum physicist friend, Phil, explains, *"It doesn't take a genius to figure that, as everything was created at the same time, then everything is entangled. And that includes you and me."*

The phenomenon where particles like Bob and Alice, millions of light years apart, dance in perfect step, regardless of time or distance, is known as "nonlocality".

What more proof do we need that everything is connected?

For 2600 years the Buddhists have been saying that all life is connected, and you are part of it.

Aboriginal cultures know it. To quote Dr Bruce Lipton, *"Aboriginal cultures do not make the usual distinctions between rocks, air and humans; all are imbued with spirit, the invisible energy. Doesn't this sound familiar? This is the world of quantum physics in which matter and energy are completely entangled."* [41]

This is the Universe we live in. We take radio waves and ultrasound for granted. And microwaves – isn't it amazing that you can be standing in a solid steel elevator and take a phone call from your mother? How does your Mum get through solid steel?

Humans are simply sophisticated transmitters and receivers. Edison and Einstein had no doubts about that.

Parts Reflecting the Whole

The idea of every tiny part being connected to the whole is not new. Here are some examples.

- Holograms – those 3D images that we often see on credit cards and software packages. You may have, for example, an image of an eagle. The *entire image* is in every part of the hologram. If you smash the hologram into a thousand pieces, you get a thousand complete little images of an eagle.
- Every cell in your body contains the DNA blueprint for your entire body.

Remember Professor Wolfgang Pauli's Exclusion Principle – elements throughout the Universe are continually adjusting and responding to each other? What does this resemble?

It resembles how a single cell works. It resembles how the 50 trillion cells in your body cooperate. It resembles the *Gaia* effect – how the Earth continues to bring itself back into balance.

A hundred years ago Nobel Prize winner and originator of quantum physics, Max Planck, discovered that *a vacuum isn't a vacuum*. Empty space is actually a *hive of activity*.

If the Universe is actually a hive of roaring activity and there is no such thing as empty space, then everything IS connected to everything else.

In a Nutshell

The whole Universe is a living, breathing, conscious thing.
We could call it universal consciousness.

Inspiration

20

How often does this happen to you? You have been trying to figure out what to say in a speech or wondering where to find a missing file. You are sitting on the toilet – you are not even trying to solve the problem – when out of the blue, you know the answer.

Or maybe you've spent weeks wondering what to buy your Mum for her birthday. You are soaping yourself in the shower, and bingo! You get the perfect solution!

Such solutions pop out of your subconscious mind. We touched on this earlier.

The subconscious mind only engages when we are relaxed – and for many of us, one of the few times we relax is on the toilet. In fact, you have to relax to get the job done!

It is the job of the conscious mind to pose the problem, to set the goal. Beyond that, the conscious mind is of limited value.

All of us are open to inner guidance and inspiration. We can each access help from a source higher than our physical selves. Whether you are comfortable with words like *God, Source* or *infinite wisdom* is not an issue. But you need to be *seriously asking* and *seriously listening*. Inner communication is like regular communication between people. To get help, you need to be open to it.

The Problem with Ego

Imagine that I wanted to get to the train station and I stopped you in the street to say, *"Can you tell me which way to the train station? Actually, I do know the way and I have found my own way there before very successfully, and I have some good reasons why I'm here and not there yet, and I don't really need anyone's help, but I'm curious to see if you know as much as me. I'm doing fine, actually, and I can find it by myself."*

Would you help me get to the station? Not likely.

I'm justifying all my actions. I already have all the answers and I'm not listening, anyway. My ego is in the way.

But what if I had been wandering the streets for three days and I staggered toward you, thirsty and exhausted, and said, *"How do I get to the station?"*

Now I'm hungry for information. I'm making no excuses. I'm beyond worrying about what you think of me. My ego is out of the way. I'm in a state of complete non-resistance. Now I'm listening. Now you can help me.

In everyday life we can receive help only when we are open to it. So it is with inner guidance, inspiration and intuition.

So do you have to be on your knees before you get inspiration? Not at all. The easiest way to get inspiration is by being happy and grateful. That's when life flows, that's when you get ideas when you need them, and that's when you keep finding yourself in the right place at the right time.

The way to choke everything off is to be upset, angry and depressed. While we are arguing with everything and insisting that the *world is wrong*, while we are full of excuses, our mind is too distracted to even notice any help.

In a Nutshell

It makes no difference whether you are a Christian, a Muslim, a Buddhist, a Scientologist, an atheist or a communist; whoever you are, you can ask for help and get it.

Will I Hear a Voice from the Sky?

When you are overwhelmed and distressed, your best strategy is to say, "Please show me the next step." If you are humble enough and open enough to say, "Just show me what I need to do today," and ask for the same help tomorrow, you can find your way out of the hole.

Let's say that you are flat-broke. You've lost your job, you're hungry, your car has been repossessed

> *The easiest way to get inspiration is by being happy and grateful.*

and you are facing eviction. You see no way out and so you decide to ask for divine guidance.

Now, to you, the ideal solution may be first prize in a $50 million lottery – but solutions may come in other ways. Very likely, help will be more of an unfolding process. Help doesn't mean that *everything is fixed for us*. *Help* means assistance and direction.

Ask and you will be shown, but usually, it won't be a voice from the sky. It could be that a friend calls with a helpful suggestion. It could be that you are led to a book or a magazine article. It could be that for no known reason, you turn to a TV channel you never watch and see an advertisement you never saw before.

Often we receive help and never recognise it. So we say, "It wasn't divine inspiration. It was actually my old friend Ted who showed up unexpectedly." In fact, Ted was a part of a miraculous process.

In a Nutshell
If we only ask, we find help and guidance. As we make it a habit to silently give thanks, help and guidance come more and more often.

Finding Your Wallet, Finding Answers
How often do you lose something – your keys, your wallet, your phone – and search desperately, without luck. Eventually you give up. You say to yourself, "If I quit looking, I will find it."

You abandon your desperate search and get on with your day. And then, within minutes, and for absolutely no reason, you decide to shift a cushion on the sofa and there, wedged into the armrest, is your wallet.

The secret to finding solutions in your life is a lot like finding your wallet. You say to yourself, "I want to find it. I will find it," and then you quit banging your head against a wall. You let go.

Needing Doesn't Help
Wanting is an important part of the process. But it is a relaxed kind of *wanting* – not a desperate "this is ruining my life" kind of *needing*.

Here is an important distinction: the feeling of *needing* is totally different from the feeling of *wanting*. Needing is more like a *hopeless desperation*. When you need something, your attention is on what you *don't have*. And when you focus on what you don't have, you will continue not to have it.

Wanting is more often a *happy anticipation*. When you want something, you are focused on what you *will have*. That is why you get it.

Songwriters and inventors will often say, "The idea just came to me." Perhaps you have thought, "How come brilliant ideas don't come to me? I would like to invent something! I would like to write a hit song." When you really, really want ideas and inspiration, they do come.

Singer and songwriter, Carole King, has written over 100 hit songs. Says Carole, "When I'm truly present, I get out of the way and all this stuff comes through." Sir Paul McCartney, ex-Beatle and writer of the most recorded pop tune ever, said that the melody for "Yesterday" came to him in a dream. You say, "What a lucky guy! He takes a nap and wakes up having written the most popular tune in history. I'd like to do that!"

But there is more to it. Here is a man whose every waking moment was dedicated to writing beautiful music. He spent his life putting phrases and melodies together and pulling them apart. When you love your work that much – and when you ask your subconscious for help – you get answers.

The other half of the story is that Paul spent *months* writing the lyrics. So sometimes you get flashes of inspiration and sometimes you need to roll up your sleeves.

In a Nutshell

The secret to finding solutions – creative solutions, financial solutions, relationship solutions – is twofold. You have to want it, and your mind needs to be in a relaxed state of anticipation.

So How Does All This "Feelings" Information Fit with Spirituality?

It fits perfectly. It explains spirituality perfectly.

It explains why all the great spiritual teachings have love (feeling) as their foundation. Whether you are Hindu, Sikh, Taoist, Christian, Muslim or Jewish, you simply EMBRACE YOUR SPIRITUAL BELIEFS SO THAT YOU FEEL AS GOOD AS YOU POSSIBLY CAN, ALWAYS.

You might say, "But I'm not spiritual."

If you can delight in watching a baby sleep, if you can be transfixed by a mountain view, if you have ever been entranced by an elephant or a hummingbird, if you find joy in paddling a canoe or wonder in the eyes of a German Shepherd or a whale, you are spiritual.

The life force that holds together a diamond, the life force that runs through an oak tree or a kitten, is the same life force that runs through you and me.

You can't help being spiritual. The Universe is coursing through you; spirit is in you.

> **The first peace, which is the most important, is that which comes within the souls of people when they realise their relationship, their oneness with the universe and all its powers, and when they realise at the centre of the universe dwells the Great Spirit, and that this centre is really everywhere, it is within each of us.**
> **Black Elk, Sioux Medicine Man**

In his classic book, *The Autobiography of a Yogi*, Paramahansa Yogananda[42] tells the story of his search for a guru. His quest begins at the age of twelve. He travels thousands of miles around India and eventually finds his master living almost next door.

Yogananda's story is every man's story.

We long to connect with the power of the Universe. We join groups, do seminars and scale mountains in Tibet. We visit cathedrals and make pilgrimages. But we don't really need to go anywhere:

> **You do not need to leave your room. Remain sitting at your table and listen. Do not even listen, simply wait, be quiet, still and solitary. The world will freely offer itself to you to be unmasked, it has no choice, it will roll in ecstasy at your feet**
> **Franz Kafka**

In a Nutshell

You are not separate from anything. You don't have to go anywhere to find the power of the Universe.

You find it by feeling different.

TOM ALWAYS DREAMED OF BEING A MILLIONAIRE

ONE DAY WHILE OUT IN HIS LITTLE BOAT

HE WAS HIT BY A HUGE STORM.

BLOWN THOUSANDS OF MILES OFF COURSE, TOM WAS FINALLY WASHED ONTO AN ISLAND

WHERE HE FOUND A TRUNK

FULL OF MONEY!

TOM HAD REALISED HIS DREAM.

ANDREW MATTHEWS

A Better Way to Achieve Goals

21

Does achieving goals make us happy? According to Mother Teresa, not necessarily. She said, "More tears are shed over answered prayers than unanswered ones."

Did you ever chase something and GET it – a pay rise, a degree, a trophy – and it didn't make you as happy as you had hoped?

So is there a problem with setting goals? No, there is sometimes a problem with HOW we set goals.

Choosing Specific Goals

There are two problems with choosing *specific* goals …

The FIRST PROBLEM: When you fix your mind on a specific wife, car or job, you are choosing based only on what you can see. So you limit yourself. You can't possibly know whether it is the *best option for you*.

And the SECOND PROBLEM? When you fix your mind on something, it is very hard to remain unattached and happy. You keep thinking, "Is somebody else going to grab my car, job, apartment or future husband before I do?"

So if we want to be happy, does goal-setting need to be more complicated?"

Actually, it needs to be simpler.

The Solution

There are basically two ways to pursue our dreams. The HARD WAY …

This is when we say, "I know best!" We choose very specific goals: I must have THAT girl, THAT job, THAT car. I must get on THAT flight. We sometimes achieve our goal, but we are regularly disappointed.

The EASY way is to be less specific …

Let's say you think you have found the perfect car, job, apartment, vacation package. It SEEMS to be the answer to your prayers. What do you do? You begin to feel your goal happily achieved, and here is what you tell yourself:

- "that car OR SOMETHING BETTER".
- "that apartment OR SOMETHING BETTER."
- "the perfect man for me – WHOEVER HE IS."

"They're not happy. They just think
they're happy."

This way of thinking becomes your way of life.

The magic is that you are unattached. You accept that your conscious mind can only see a fraction of the picture.

- Before you book a flight, you see and feel yourself travelling on the perfect flight – and you let things unfold
- Before making an appointment with a doctor, dentist, accountant, you see and feel yourself finding the perfect professional – and you let things unfold
- Before you hire a secretary, book a vacation, attend an interview, go on a date, you feel it as unfolding perfectly.

You don't try to figure it all out. You just know that you are connected to everything and that when you are calm and when you believe in the process, it works.

The Secret

The Indian guru, J Krishnamurti, once gave a lecture. Midway through his talk he stopped. He asked his audience, "Do you want to know what my secret is?"

The hall went silent. Everyone leaned forward. Everyone wanted to know. Krishnamurti continued, "This is my secret: I don't mind what happens."

This is the secret to goal-setting.

- You feel good
- You picture the perfect result for you
- You take whatever action seems necessary, moment by moment
- You don't mind what happens.

You say, "Andrew, it took us a hundred pages to get to this point! Now you say, 'Feel good and don't care what happens!'." That's right. The best answers are SIMPLE.

Spiritual teachers often use the example of the acorn. The acorn has the idea of the beautiful oak inside it. It doesn't struggle to be a tree.

It is the same with us. We are born with the idea of a beautiful life inside us. Struggling doesn't help.

In a Nutshell

The hard way is forcing things to happen.
The easy way is allowing things to happen.

A Sketch of How Life Works

22

This is where we have come so far. Here is a sketch of *how life works*:

- NOTHING IN THIS UNIVERSE IS REALLY SOLID (proven by 100 years of quantum physics experiments) which means:
- EVERYTHING IS ENERGY (demonstrated by Albert Einstein's famous $e = mc^2$) and
- MATTER IS REALLY CRYSTALLISED THOUGHT
- THOUGHTS AFFECT MATTER (beautifully illustrated by Dr Masaru Emoto and his crystals)
- WHEN ONE TINY ELECTRON CHANGES ITS SPIN, CHANGES REVERBERATE ACROSS THE UNIVERSE (as proven by Professor Wolfgang Pauli), which proves EVERYTHING IS CONNECTED.

This all sounds beyond belief – but then, so is the concept of creation or a Big Bang.

A Universe that is expanding at the speed of light is also beyond belief – and so is the fact that there are 300,000,000,000,000,000,000,000,000,000 things happening in your body every second.

It is all miraculous, including the fact that:

- YOUR SUBCONSCIOUS STORES ALL THE THOUGHTS AND FEELINGS THAT YOU HAVE EVER HAD (which is why hypnosis digs up old memories)
- Because everything is connected, YOUR SUBCONSCIOUS IS CONNECTED TO EVERYTHING. This explains why:
- YOUR SUBCONSCIOUS MIND CREATES YOUR LIFE EXPERIENCE.

The good news is:

- FEELINGS REPROGRAM YOUR SUBCONSCIOUS
- WHEN YOU FEEL DIFFERENT, YOU CHANGE YOUR DESTINY.

You are responsible for your life experience. You are creating your life, moment by moment.

You Always Knew It

So what is the formula for success and happiness?

- Live with joy and enthusiasm
- Use your imagination to create vivid pictures of what you want
- Persist toward your goals in a light-hearted happy way
- Live without fear and prejudice
- Let go of disappointments
- Forgive in a heartbeat
- Love for no reason.

You say, "Be real! Who lives like that?"

And the answer is: "Three-year-old children."

You arrived here programmed for success. At three, you knew how life works.

Jesus said, *"Except ye be converted and become as little children, ye shall not enter into the kingdom of heaven."* [43]

What do you think he is talking about?

Heaven is not a chunk of real estate for dead people somewhere between Venus and Uranus. Heaven is a state of mind. Heaven is a state of being where life unfolds miraculously.

In a Nutshell

Fortunately, you don't have to remember any quantum physics. Just study the three-year-old masters.

Will Success Make Me Happy?

No. You have to be happy first. You have to like yourself first.

If you are miserable before a promotion, you will be miserable after a promotion. If you feel worthless without a million dollars, you will feel worthless with a million dollars. If life is empty without a boyfriend, life will be empty with a boyfriend.

Achieving goals won't make you happy. You need to like yourself when you are *not achieving*!

In a Nutshell
The world believes, "Success makes you happy." The truth is; happiness makes you successful.

The Happier You Get ...
This morning I was interviewed on radio. The host, Sara, shared her own story with the listeners. She explained:

> "Five years ago, I was unhappy. My boyfriend is always happy.
>
> "My boyfriend works with refugees at the YMCA. He helps to build their confidence and helps them to start new lives. So he is a positive guy who looks on the bright side.
>
> "Whenever I used to complain about something, he would say, *'What is one good thing about it?'* If I was unhappy about having to work on a weekend, he would ask me, *'What is good about working on a weekend? There is less traffic. It means you have a job.'*
>
> "He constantly encouraged me to look for good things. At first, it was irritating. I found it hard to change my thinking. But it got easier to see the positive side. I was happier. Eventually, looking for good things became a habit.
>
> "Now that I feel so much happier, I can't believe how lucky I get!"

"Now that I feel so much happier, I can't believe how lucky I get!"

Sara's experience is this book in a nutshell. At first, it can be hard to find reasons to be happy. But it gets easier. You gather momentum and the better you feel, the "luckier" you get.

For those of us who don't have Sara's boyfriend to coach us, the next three chapters share three simple principles that change everything.

Sometimes I ask myself,
"Why am I the lucky one?"

Be Grateful

23

**If the only prayer you ever say in your entire life
is "Thank you", it will be enough.**
Meister Eckhart

As a kid I often asked the question, "If God is so wonderful, why would He care if we say thank you? Why give thanks at mealtimes? What is the point of those bedtime prayers: *'Thank you for Mummy and Daddy and a warm bed.'*? Why is gratitude important?"

Why did Abraham, Zoroaster, Lao Tzu, Buddha, Jesus Christ, Mohammed, Yogananda and my Mum all recommend being thankful? And why is it that so many people make time for *gratitude journals*?

> *"When I'm happy, then I'll be grateful!"*

It's because gratitude changes you. There is no faster way to elevate your vibration. Gratitude is the fast track to the life you want.

The more often that you have the feeling, *"I have what I want"*, the more often you get what you want. Appreciation is as good as meditation.

How do you practise gratitude? Here are simple things any six-year-old can do.

EACH NIGHT: As you go to sleep, review your day and make a list of everything you are thankful for: family, friends, sunshine, medication, deodorant, your laptop, a safe flight, a great lunch, a laugh with a neighbour, a walk with your dog, stars …

EACH MORNING: Give thanks for one more day.

KEEP A GRATITUDE JOURNAL: Make lists of everything that you are thankful for and keep adding to it.

MAKE A GRATITUDE BOARD: I have a pinboard by my desk. It is covered with about 50 photographs of family and friends I love the most, photographs of places Julie and I have enjoyed the most, highlights of vacations and events for which I feel blessed. I look at it every day and tell myself, "I AM so lucky!" I put it together when I was feeling stuck and not very grateful.

A gratitude board is a joy to make. And here's the key – each time you look at it, be sure to say "I AM so fortunate," and not "How happy I WAS."

"When I was your age I was proud to
be seen with my parents!"

GIVE THANKS FOR EVERY SMALL THING: Whatever gives you joy –
dogs at play, a glass of clean water, a hug from your wife – make it a habit to say
a silent "thank you". If a stranger gives you a smile, say a silent, "thank you".
If you are broke and you find a dollar, say "thank you". Gratitude for even tiny
things makes you a magnet for more good things.

WHEN THINGS SEEM TO BE GOING WRONG: Ask yourself, "What
is one good thing about this disaster?" And if you can find nothing good, say
"thank you", anyway: "I have no idea how this could possibly be good, but
'thank you' in advance."

Once you understand that gratitude transforms lives, you become a *gratitude warrior*.

Once you believe that nothing is an accident and every event is helping you
on your journey, you give thanks for everything. That's when the Universe really
starts plotting to make you happy.

In a Nutshell

Average people say: "When I'm *happy,* then I'll be *grateful.*"
Joyful people say: "When I'm *grateful,* then I'll be *happy.*"

Living in the Now

24

Why is it that we are so obsessed with *finding* love, *keeping* love or *getting it back?*

Of course, love feels wonderful. For example, Ted meets Poppy. For the first time he has found someone who doesn't want to change him (yet). And he doesn't want to change her. "Poppy, you are my princess! You are perfect just as you are!" When Ted is in Princess Poppy's arms, he wants nothing else; he wants to be nowhere else.

Is it that Poppy is so wonderful? Obviously! And it is also this: for the first time in his life Ted is totally happy with the present moment. For thirty years he has been consumed by the belief that "I should be better. I should be richer, smarter, taller. Once I get this, once I become that, I'll be okay." But when he is with Poppy, everything is perfect.

Love is seeing the best in ourselves reflected. Love is a window onto the beauty of humanity. And love is a window into the present moment.

When Ted has that rush of joy, that boundless, breathless energy that fills his being, he thinks it's POPPY. His friends think he is on DRUGS. It is actually Ted embracing the PRESENT MOMENT.

When you fall in love, you have no resistance. You are no longer trying to fix anything or change anyone. You are not judging, hiding or wishing you were any place else. You become a pure channel for universal energy.

In a Nutshell

When you find love, you are in the present.
And if you can find the present, you find love.

You Have No Future!

Self-help gurus and Zen Buddhists tell us to *live in the present,* but does it matter? It matters. Because when you are happy, enthusiastic, absorbed, in love, you plug into the power of the Universe. When you are

dissatisfied, distracted and depressed, you are unplugged – and when you are unplugged, you are powerless to create anything better.

Your key to a better life is to feel good *now*. Not next week, not when you pay off the apartment, not when peace is declared in the Middle East. Every moment that you spend regretting the past or fearing the future is an affirmation that life is lousy – and so you get more of "lousy".

> The two most powerful words in the universe are, "I AM".

Here's another reason to live in the present: the future doesn't exist. *You have no future!* Of course, we pretend it does. We pretend that time is like a piece of string where the past is on one end, the future is on the other end, and the present is in the middle. Not so.

All we have is an eternally unfolding present moment. The only time you will ever meet the future is when it becomes NOW. And when the future is now, it is not the future.

Why even talk about this? Because it explains why some people who imagine a wonderful future stay stuck in a crappy present. There is no value in waiting for something that doesn't exist. It is useless telling yourself "I WILL BE rich, I WILL BE happy, I WILL BE successful." When your mind is in the future you are spinning your wheels.

Your power is in the present: "I AM rich. I AM happy. I AM successful." What did God say to Moses? "I AM that I AM." It's no coincidence. God gets it. The two most powerful words in the Universe are, "I AM".

Some people live their life like they are stranded in a wasteland: "One day I'll find my way out of this hell and my life will start." No! You escape by gathering happy thoughts NOW. How so? Because problems exist *in the future*. Unless you are having a heart attack or being eaten by a bear, your present moment is usually fine. It is the imaginary future that drives you nuts: "What will happen if? How will I survive if? What will other people say?"

You are perfectly designed to handle present moments. You conquer worry by dragging your mind back to the present. You remind yourself, "Right this second I have everything I need. I choose to enjoy THIS moment." Every second that you live in the present moment is an affirmation that life is good – and that "feeling goodness" showers more goodness on you.

Your life will work to the extent that you can say:

- there is nothing I need other than this moment
- there is no one I need to impress and no one I need to become
- I am what I am
- I have everything I need to be happy.

In a Nutshell
The answer to the big question, "What should I do with my future?" is "Live in the present".

Love Yourself

25

Be Gentle with Yourself

There is one danger in accepting that you create your life experience: once you acknowledge that you are responsible for how your life has unfolded, you may want to beat yourself up! You may ask yourself, "How could I have been so stupid?" You may blame yourself or even hate yourself. This is a really bad idea!

Here's a better way to talk to yourself:

- "I have been living life the best way I know how."
- "Now that I know better, I will think and feel differently."
- "Now that I know better, I will do better."

Congratulate yourself on surviving to this point. NO SHAME. NO BLAME.

Why Loving Yourself Matters

Every experience you will ever have is coloured by HOW YOU FEEL ABOUT YOU. Every thought, every conversation, every waking moment, every dreaming moment is shaped by whether you love, hate, blame or forgive yourself.

So now we get to the heart of the matter. Because:

- the life you create depends on how you feel
- there will never be a time in your life when *you are not present* (because wherever you go, you are always there!)

EVERYTHING THAT HAPPENS IN YOUR LIFE DEPENDS ON HOW YOU FEEL ABOUT YOU.

TO CONTINUOUSLY HAVE GOOD THINGS HAPPENING IN YOUR LIFE, YOU HAVE TO LOVE YOURSELF – not in some arrogant, conceited or boastful way, but in an accepting, compassionate, good-humoured way.

People who love and accept themselves are energetic and optimistic. They are healthier. They have their challenges, but they don't take problems personally. Things always seem to work out. People who blame and berate themselves live lives of struggle and desperation.

The evidence is everywhere. It doesn't matter how much you know. FOR YOUR LIFE TO WORK, YOU HAVE TO LOVE YOU.

"But how can I love myself?"

Buddha gives us some encouragement:

> **You can search throughout the entire universe for someone who is more deserving of your love and affection than you are yourself, and that person is not to be found anywhere. You yourself, as much as anybody in the entire universe deserve your love and affection.**
> *Buddha*

What Can You Do?

FOCUS ON YOUR GOOD POINTS: Quit looking at what you don't like about yourself. Concentrate on what you like about you, and the bad stuff will drop away. What you focus on expands.

ALWAYS SPEAK WELL OF YOURSELF: Never criticise yourself. It is self-sabotage and it irritates people. If you have nothing good to say about yourself, say nothing.

LOOK FOR GOOD THINGS IN OTHER PEOPLE: People who feel bad about themselves search for faults in others. The flip side is: look for qualities in others and you will feel better about yourself.

LOOK FOR BEAUTY EVERYWHERE: To recognise beauty within a flower, a cathedral, a rock, a sunset, a puppy, you have to have it within you. Otherwise, you wouldn't know it when you saw it.

Appreciation of everything around us leads us to self-love.

TAKE CARE OF YOUR HOME: Where you live affects how you feel. Create a space that will uplift you when you walk in the front door. Neatness costs nothing. Better to live in a one-room apartment that is clean than in a mansion that's a mess. Your home may not be grand but it can be tidy! Hang pictures or photographs that inspire you.

Fred says, "When I get successful, I'll quit living like a rat." Wrong! To be a success you have to begin to live well. You have to feel good now.

NURTURE YOURSELF: Firstly, here's what nurturing yourself is NOT.

Lisa, who is a month behind in her rent and owes ten grand on her credit cards, buys a two-thousand-dollar handbag and proclaims, "I deserve it!" No, Lisa! Blowing big money you *don't have* on stuff you *don't need is* not *nurturing* yourself; it's *punishing* yourself.

Nurturing yourself is doing things that make you feel good that *you can afford.* Here's what it might mean:

- If you are flat-broke: walking in a city park and enjoying the flowers; sitting in the foyer of a beautiful five-star hotel and reading a book (it's free); learning massage online with a friend and spoiling each other with a relaxing treatment once a week.
- If you have some spare dollars: buying an economy air ticket and using points to upgrade to business class for the first time in your life; saving ten dollars a week until you can afford to take your Mum to lunch at the best restaurant in town.

Make it your mission to enjoy affordable pleasures. Start now. Nurturing yourself means spending time with people who uplift you. It means seeking out sweet experiences, stretching your expectations and feeling better and better, bit by bit.

MEDITATE: The purpose of meditation is TO BE without purpose. We are so busy "*doing*", we often forget to be human "*beings*". Meditation is the ultimate exercise in detachment and feeling good.

LEARN TO RECEIVE: Maybe you have a friend like Mary.

- You invite her to dinner. She says, "Don't go to any trouble."
- You buy her a birthday present. She says, "You shouldn't have."
- You offer to carry her groceries. She says, "I can manage."
- You tell her she's beautiful and she says, "I've got a fat butt."

Maybe you are like Mary. If you want a rich life, learn to accept other people's help, invitations, gifts and compliments happily.

DO THINGS YOU LOVE: Spend time doing things you love – if not in your work time, then in your spare time. If you love music, or painting or swimming with sharks, make time for it. When you do things you love, you affirm, "I am worth it and what I care about matters."

> *Get comfortable with receiving.*

BE GENTLE WITH YOURSELF: If you find it difficult to love or forgive yourself, get a photograph of yourself aged two, or four, and put it on your desk. It is much easier to forgive a four-year-old.

We love our husbands, wives, parents, boyfriends and *they're not perfect*. So why should you have to be perfect? Tell yourself, "I don't have to be perfect – and that's perfect".

GIVE YOURSELF CREDIT: A happy life is about improvement, not perfection. Celebrate small steps of progress.

In a Nutshell

Love yourself.
Your life depends on it.

HAPPY PEOPLE FOCUS ON WHAT THEY <u>HAVE</u>

UNHAPPY PEOPLE FOCUS ON WHAT'S MISSING.

Why Am I Here?

26

"Why am I here?"

Happiness is the meaning and the purpose of life,
the whole aim and end of human existence.
Aristotle

Imagine for a moment that you were God and you decided to make some humans.

These humans are like apprentice creators. They don't build universes, but they are fairly handy. They write stories and make music, invent helicopters and iPods, build cities and also make babies.

If you were God, how would you design things? Would you organise it so that these humans were helpless victims of fate – and what would be the point? Or would you design a world where humans could gradually realise their own power to create their own life experiences? How would this be for a scheme?

These humans inhabit a Universe that seems solid enough. But on investigation they discover that the building blocks of the Universe are not solid particles but waves of energy. This energy turns out to be the same stuff as human thoughts.

In this Universe, the mission of every human is to take total responsibility for his life by controlling his thoughts and feelings.

Do you like this idea? I hope so, because this is our Universe.

Edgar Mitchell, the Apollo astronaut, put it in a nutshell:

> **If we change our heads about who we are – and can see ourselves as creative, eternal beings creating physical experience, joined at that level of existence we call consciousness – then we start to see and create this world that we live in quite differently.**[44]

The spiritual Masters have always taught this. Some people are born knowing it. Science is catching up.

Does it sound too fantastic – that with our thoughts and feelings we create our life experience? The evidence is all around us. We come here to discover our own power. We are neither victims nor pawns. We are creators.

You have probably always sensed this. You are not some leaf in the wind. You control your destiny.

The Big Questions

Too often we focus on our differences. What is the *difference* between men and women? What is the *difference* between my religion and your religion?

But imagine for a moment that we gathered some spiritual masters – Jesus, Buddha, Mohammed, Lao Tzu – and asked them to answer some big questions. I am guessing that they would all agree on the answers.

What am I?

You are a spark of God, or *Source*. Your essence is love. The rest is illusion or wrong thinking.

What is My Goal?

To think like God thinks. To love like God loves. To create like God creates.

In Summary

You are a spirit having a physical experience. Whatever shows up in your life – joy, abundance, ulcers, the FBI – is precise feedback on what your thoughts and feelings have created.

At some stage the penny will drop that you are entirely responsible for your reality. Until you *get it,* life can be hell on Earth.

After you *get it,* life becomes a game in which:

- your dreams move toward you with increasing speed
- everything becomes more and more fun.

The major rules of the game are:

- ACCEPT – yourself, others and your current situation
- FORGIVE – yourself and others
- BE GRATEFUL
- LIVE IN THE MOMENT
- FEEL YOUR GOALS ALREADY ACHIEVED
- REPLACE FEAR WITH LOVE AND KINDNESS
- BE HAPPY.

Living with these guidelines, you raise your energy and steadily become more powerful. You achieve *more and more* with *less effort.* You also realise that it is not actually you that is doing it. The power comes *through* you.

No one is holding you back. No one can hold you back.

You don't need more information. You don't need more seminars or anyone's permission. You just refine each piece of the puzzle in your own time and know that it is perfect.

In a Nutshell

Your mission is to FEEL AS GOOD AS POSSIBLE EVERY MINUTE, EVERY HOUR, EVERY DAY. That is how life works.

References

1 Hill, Napoleon. *Think and Grow Rich*. Cleveland, Ohio: The Ralston Publishing Co, 1953.

2 Maltz, Maxwell. Psycho-Cybernetics. Pocket Books, 1989.

3 Bristol, Claude M. *The Magic of Believing: The Science of Setting Your Goal and Then Reaching It.* Fireside, 1991.

4 Peale, Norman V. *The Power of Positive Thinking*. Fawcett Columbine, 1952.

5 Photographs reproduced by permission of Dr Masaru Emoto.

6 McTaggart, Lynne. *The Intention Experiment*. Free Press, 2007, p 24.

7 Rein, Glen and McCraty, Rollin. Structural changes in water and DNA associated with new physiologically measurable states. *Journal of Scientific Exploration*. 1994; 8(3): 438-439.

8 Eddington, Arthur. *The Nature of the Physical World*. Macmillan, 1935.

9 Hawking, Stephen: *Into the Universe*, Series 1: Episode 3 (4:16)

10 Gawain, Shakti. *Creative Visualisation*, Whatever Publishing, 1978 pages 8 and 10.

11 Goddard, Neville. *Feeling is the Secret*. BN Publishing, 2007, page 19.

12 Douglas-Klotz, Neil (trans). *Prayers of the Cosmos: Meditations on the Aramaic Words of Jesus*. San Francisco: Harper, 1994, p. 86-87.

13 Braden, Gregg. *Secrets of the Lost Mode of Prayer*. Hay House, 2006, pp 7-8.

14 Matthew, 13:12.

15 Goddard, Neville. *Feeling is the Secret*. BN Publishing , 2007, pages 16 and 21.

16 Pauli, Wolfgang. Relation between the closing in of electron-groups in the atom and the structure of complexes in the spectrum. *Zeitschrift fur Physik*. 1925; 31: 765-783.

17 Hill, Napoleon. *Think and Grow Rich*. Cleveland, Ohio: The Ralston Publishing Co, 1953.

18 Fictional characters from George Lucas's film, *Star Wars*, 1977.

19 *The Voice*, Nine Network Television, Australia, 2013.

20 Matthews, Andrew. *Being Happy!* Media Masters, Singapore, 1988.

21 Jim Carrey. Interview in *Movieline*, July, 1994.

22 Matthews, Andrew. *Being Happy!* Media Masters, Singapore, 1988.

23 Matthew 5:39.

24 Foundation for Inner Peace. *A Course in Miracles*. 2nd ed. New York: Viking Penguin, 1996. Lesson 243.

25 Brown, Brené PhD, *The Power of Vulnerability*, www.ted.com/talks/brene_brown_on_ vulnerability

26 Moseley, J. Bruce, et al. A controlled trial for arthroscopic surgery of the knee, *New England Journal of Medicine*, 2002; 347: 81-88.

27 Moseley, Bruce. *60 Minutes* interview, 29 November, 2012.

28 Lipton, Bruce. *The Biology of Belief: Unleashing the Power of Consciousness, Matter & Miracles*. Hay House, 2011.

29 Ibid, p. 42.

30 Pert, Candace. *Molecules of Emotion*. Simon and Schuster, 1997, p 189.

31 Pearsall, Paul. *The Heart's Code*. Broadway, 1998, p 65.

32 Ibid.

33 Ibid.

34 Sylvia, Claire. *A Change of Heart*. Warner Books, 1998.

35 Pearsall, Paul. *The Heart's Code*. Broadway, 1998, p 7.

36 Orme-Johnson D, Alexander C, Davies J, Chandler H, Larimore W. International Peace Project in the Middle East: The effects of the Maharishi Technology of the Unified Field. *Journal of Conflict Resolution*. 1988; 32(4): 776-812.

37 International Peace Project in the Middle East: The Effects of Maharishi Technology of the Unified Field. *The Journal of Conflict Resolution,* Vol 32, No 4, Dec. 1988.

38 Byrd, R C, Ph.D., Positive therapeutic effects of intercessory prayer in a coronary care unit population. *Southern Medical Journal*. 1988; 81: 826-829.

39 McTaggart, Lynne. *The Intention Experiment*. Free Press, 2007, p 23.

40 The Secret Life of Plants, Part 2 of 4, interview with Cleve Backster, http://www.youtube.com/watch?v=nYksxtB0w8U , (0:47)

41 Lipton, Bruce H. *The Biology of Belief*. Hay House, 2005, pp 155.

42 Yogananda, Paramahansa. *Autobiography of a Yogi*. Self-Realization Fellowship, 1948.

43 Matthew 18:3.

44 Mitchell, Edgar. As the paradigm shifts: Two decades of consciousness research. *Noetic Sciences Review*. 1992; 24: p.7.

READERS' COMMENTS

I was bed-ridden with terrible depression, my childhood was getting me down, my business was struggling. Then I read your books.

It has completely changed my life. I began exercising my body and mind. I now run a national consultancy business. I now appreciate each day. I am so grateful.

Adam Sanderson, Woore, U.K.

"Your books gave me a light when I was totally in darkness. They changed me and my view of life. Now, your books have become a kind of Bible for me … I want to express my REAL, DEEP APPRECIATION for your books and your message."

Moonsun Choi, KOREA

"Your books have already changed my life! They are so simple and straightforward that anyone can put them into practice immediately. I am now much happier and more self-confident. Thank you!"

Szymon Przedwojski, POLAND

"Your books do wonderful things. I always hated myself because I failed at exams. It was difficult for me to make friends. Now my life has changed and no words can describe my happiness. Thank you."

Nguyen Duc An Khanh, VIETNAM

I found your books about five years ago when I was in a desperate situation: father had a heart attack, my husband had a bad accident, Mum diagnosed with carcinoma, and to complete the disaster, I lost my job – all within three months!

Reading your books was like a helping hand. One moment I was drowning, and then suddenly I felt safe. Thank you so very much!

Rosanna Monaco, Zurich, SWITZERLAND

Andrew Matthews: Speaker

Andrew Matthews speaks to conferences worldwide.

Andrew has addressed over a thousand international corporations on five continents.

He speaks to banks, hospitals, government institutions, IT corporations and prisons, and he has addressed more than 500 universities and schools around the world.

Andrew's topics include:

- attitude
- dealing with disasters
- embracing change
- life/ work balance
- prosperity and success.

Contact:

For enquiries and to engage Andrew Matthews:
Email:info@seashell.com.au
Tel: +61 740 556 966
www.andrewmatthews.com

WATKINS

Sharing Wisdom Since 1893

The story of Watkins began in 1893, when scholar of esotericism John Watkins founded our bookshop, inspired by the lament of his friend and teacher Madame Blavatsky that there was nowhere in London to buy books on mysticism, occultism or metaphysics. That moment marked the birth of Watkins, soon to become the publisher of many of the leading lights of spiritual literature, including Carl Jung, Rudolf Steiner, Alice Bailey and Chögyam Trungpa.

Today, the passion at Watkins Publishing for vigorous questioning is still resolute. Our stimulating and groundbreaking list ranges from ancient traditions and complementary medicine to the latest ideas about personal development, holistic wellbeing and consciousness exploration. We remain at the cutting edge, committed to publishing books that change lives.

DISCOVER MORE AT:

www.watkinspublishing.com

Read our blog

Watch and listen to
our authors in action

Sign up to
our mailing list

We celebrate conscious, passionate, wise and happy living.
Be part of that community by visiting

 /watkinspublishing    @watkinswisdom

 /watkinsbooks   @watkinswisdom

#0032 - 140218 - C0 - 235/180/9 - PB - 9781786781727